The End of St Petersburg

KINOfiles Film Companions
General Editor: Richard Taylor

Written for cineastes and students alike, KINOfiles are readable, authoritative, illustrated companion handbooks to the most important and interesting films to emerge from Russian cinema from its beginnings to the present. Each KINOfile investigates the production, context and reception of the film and the people who made it, and analyses the film itself and its place in Russian and world cinema. KINOfiles also include films of the other countries that once formed part of the Soviet Union, as well as works by émigré film-makers working in the Russian tradition.

KINOfiles form a part of KINO: The Russian Cinema Series.

THE END OF ST PETERSBURG

VANCE KEPLEY, Jr

KINOfiles Film Companion 10

I.B. TAURIS
LONDON · NEW YORK

Published in 2003 by I.B.Tauris & Co. Ltd
6 Salem Road, London W2 4BU
175 Fifth Avenue, New York NY 10010
www.ibtauris.com

In the United States of America and in Canada distributed by
St. Martin's Press, 175 Fifth Avenue, New York NY 10010

ISBN 1 86064 911 4

A full CIP record for this book is available from the British Library
A full CIP record for this book is available from the Library of Congress

Library of Congress catalog card: available

Set in Monotype Calisto by Ewan Smith, London
Printed and bound in Great Britain by MPG Books Ltd, Bodmin

Contents

Acknowledgements

I am very grateful to Richard Taylor for his wise editorial judgment and advice. I also thank Philippa Brewster and Susan Lawson at I.B.Tauris. Thanks to Matt Rockwell for help in preparing the final manuscript and illustrations. I am indebted to my former student Panayiota Mini, who wrote an excellent PhD dissertation on Pudovkin's silent films. I am sure that I learned more about Pudovkin from her than she did from me. As she has done so often over the years, Betty Kepley generously and patiently lent her editorial skills to this project.

This book is dedicated to my mother and father, Georgia Kepley and Vance Kepley, Sr.

Note on Transliteration

Transliteration from the Cyrillic to the Latin alphabet is a perennial problem. I have used a modification of the Library of Congress system in the text. When a Russian name has a clear English version (e.g., Alexander), or when a Russian name has an accepted English spelling (e.g., Eisenstein), I use the English. When a Russian name ends in -ii or -yi, I use a single -y for a surname (e.g., Dostoevsky instead of Dostoevskii), a single -i for a first name (Iuri instead of Iurii). In notes and bibliography I adhere to the Library of Congress system.

Production Credits

The End of St Petersburg [Konets Sankt-Peterburga]

Production Studio: Mezhrabpom (Moscow)
Director: Vsevolod Pudovkin
Co-director: Mikhail Doller
Scenario: Natan Zarkhi
Head of Cinematography: Anatoli Golovnia
Art Director: Sergei Kozlovsky
First Assistant Director: Albert Gendelshtein
Second Assistant Directors: L. Ledashchev,
    Alexander Faintsimmer, V. Straus
Camera Operator: K. Vents
Release Date: 14 December 1927
Length: 7 reels, 2,500 m

Cast

Alexander Chistiakov	The Communist Worker
Vera Baranovskaia	His Wife
Ivan Chuvelev	The Village Lad
V. Obolensky	Lebedev
A. Gromov	The Bald One
Sergei Komarov	District Police Chief
M. Tereshkovich	Reporter

V. Chuvelev	The Lad's Friend among Factory Workers
Vladimir Tsoppi	Man with Top Hat
Nikolai Khmelev, M. Tsibulsky	Stock Brokers
Vsevolod Pudovkin, Vladimir Fogel	German Officers

Introduction

Vsevolod Pudovkin holds a deserving place in the cinema pantheon as one the foremost Soviet montage directors. His 'revolutionary trilogy' of *The Mother* [Mat', 1926], *The End of St Petersburg* [Konets Sankt-Peterburga, 1927] and *Storm Over Asia* [Potomok Chingis-khana (*The Heir of Genghis-Khan*), 1928] secured his international reputation, and ensured that his name would be linked with other lionized members of the Soviet avant-garde, including Sergei Eisenstein, Dziga Vertov and Alexander Dovzhenko.

Pudovkin's reputation has long been based on something of a contradiction. He is known as the aesthetically conservative, avant-garde artist of Soviet cinema, the resident classicist among the practitioners of modernist montage. For all his innovative editing skills, his films bear the traces of time-honored storytelling practices. Whereas Vertov attacked the norms of fictional narrative, Pudovkin opted for traditional narrative designs that stressed linear causality. Whereas Eisenstein exploited social types and mass heroes instead of individual characters, Pudovkin developed psychologically detailed central characters as the bases of his dramas. Whereas Dovzhenko's editing often featured daring leaps in time and space, Pudovkin just as often practiced continuity editing, linking shots with devices that sustained orderly serial logic.

The most common way of characterizing the Soviet montage cinema is to differentiate between a conservative wing of the movement, consisting of Pudovkin and his mentor Lev Kuleshov, whose work was indebted to mainstream narrative cinema, and a more radical wing of Eisenstein, Vertov and Dovzhenko, whose work pushed more toward modernist abstraction.[1] In its most recondite form this differentiation is commonly reduced to a comparison between Eisenstein and Pudovkin. The former is usually credited with innovating a truly original, dialectical film form, and the latter is more faintly praised for reintroducing practices of classical realism into the context of the 1920s avant-garde. The two film-makers themselves encouraged such comparisons. Eisenstein identified himself with conflict-based montage in an often-cited 1929 anecdote, and he aligned Pudovkin's editing with sequential logic: 'Series–P[udovkin] and Collision–E[isenstein]'.[2] For his part, Pudovkin could extol the virtues of elliptical montage, but he also put himself on record as believing that 'continuity is essential' for films to be effective.[3]

That Eisenstein–Pudovkin differentiation does have considerable explanatory power. The distinctive features of each artist become salient through a comparison of their styles. And the cross-reference need not produce an invidious conclusion in which Eisenstein wins praise to the detriment of Pudovkin. As I will try to show in Chapter 4 of this study, Pudovkin's admirers have found ways to extol his taste for smooth linear narratives, using such terms as 'balanced', 'elegant' and even 'lyrical' to describe the films.[4]

Whatever the legitimacy of the standard characterization, it cannot apply to all of Pudovkin's films with equal measures of comfort. It may describe *The Mother* well enough, with its single protagonist and its tidy story that unfolds in carefully measured stages; but what about Pudovkin's most complex and multifarious film, *The End of St Petersburg*? This multi-dimensional masterpiece breaks the mold of that characterization. Instead of internal balance and organic unity, *The End of St Petersburg* features a diverse array of ingredients. It has several major characters and must sustain multiple sub-plots to trace out their various activities. It also contains passages from which the central characters are absent, rhetorical inserts that intentionally disrupt the narrative's flow. It switches periodically between small-scale scenes of mundane human activities and epic-scale renderings of such events as war and revolution. The plot design is highly episodic, even fragmentary, in comparison to other Pudovkin films, breaking into almost two dozen short sequences that are often separated by uncertain temporal gaps. And the film blends styles. Pudovkin might employ conventional continuity editing one moment and then abruptly move into a montage passage of highly discontinuous edits. It is precisely this mixture that is the source of the film's complexity and its aesthetic richness. In *The End of St Petersburg* Pudovkin consciously developed a mixed-mode work that takes advantage of the internal tensions among its disparate ingredients.

This brings *The End of St Petersburg* (and Pudovkin) back into the realm of the modernist avant-garde, where aesthetic eclecticism rather than organic unity was the hallmark. And it brings Pudovkin closer to Eisenstein than is normally recognized. In fact, I will argue in the following pages that *The End of St Petersburg* bears an Eisensteinian debt, partly as a result of fortuitous circumstances. Pudovkin produced *The End of St Petersburg* as an official commission to commemorate the Bolshevik Revolution's tenth anniversary (see Chapter 2). This put his project on a parallel course with Eisenstein's own commemorative film *October* [Oktiabr', 1928]. The two directors were in contact with one another while producing these equivalent projects, resulting in beneficial cross-influences. The two films even remained interconnected while in distribution; the critical reception of *The End of St Petersburg* was affected by the subsequent appearance of Eisenstein's more controversial anniversary film (see Chapter 4).

The best way to describe *The End of St Petersburg*'s aesthetic mix would be to define the two major modes from which the film borrows. Then through the course of a more extended analysis (Chapter 3), variants and combinations from those two primary categories can be more specifically treated. *The End of St Petersburg* is an example of the historical–materialist mode of filmic narration, but it also borrows heavily from the classical Hollywood mode. These two terms derive from David Bordwell's study of narration in cinema, and a brief characterization of each is in order.[5]

By the historical–materialist mode, Bordwell specifically refers to the Soviet montage films of the 1920s and early 1930s, the likes of *The Strike* [Stachka, 1925] *The Mother*, *The Arsenal* [1929], and, of course, *The End of St Petersburg*. Such films are characterized by the montage aesthetic, of course, but also by a 'strong rhetorical cast', in that they use narrational strategies for didactic purposes.[6] The process of narration does not just offer viewers story information; it also advances political arguments about the Soviet situation. In fact, the films' story material is often already familiar to viewers. Historical–materialist films commonly draw their stories from the realm of the already-known, from current events, for example, or from recent Russian history. The films' narratives then play on viewers' prior knowledge of that material. The plots may contain disjunctive elements but viewers can usually fill in background material: '[B]ecause this historical event or rhetorical point is already known, not all the links need to be shown.'[7]

The role of fictional characters in the historical–materialist mode is also distinctive. They rarely serve as narrative causal agents. Larger, impersonal social and historical forces motivate narrative actions, not the desires of particular characters. As a result, characters are defined 'chiefly through their class position, job, social actions and political views', instead of their psychological states. Rather than being individual personalities, they serve as 'prototypes of whole classes, milieus, or historical epochs'.[8] An Eisenstein character, for example, acts more in response to the collective norms of his/her social class than to private ambitions or psychological urges.

These elements of the historical–materialist mode stand in sharp contrast to the norms of the classical mode. Characters serve a primary function as agents of narrative action in classical films, and those characters are defined more by their personality traits than their social standing. Those traits explain the characters' personal ambitions and goals. Actions taken to attain those goals duly motivate narrative events. 'The principal causal agency [of narrative action] is thus the character, a discriminated individual, endowed with a consistent batch of evident traits, qualities, and behaviors.'[9]

The classical mode generally employs a film style that preserves a consistent, coherent sense of time and space for story action. Editing follows principles of continuity. Scenes often begin with a wide-view establishing shot to situate figures in space, and the space is then broken down into closer views which analyze the unfolding action. Such devices as the eyeline match (a glance followed by the object of the glance), the match on action (a movement that carries across a cut) and the shot/reverse shot design (reverse-angle shots that maintain consistent screen direction) all work together to preserve an illusion of smooth, continuous action from one shot to the next.

This classical mode is commonly associated with American commercial film-making and is frequently identified as the 'classical Hollywood cinema'.[10] In fact, its norms were developed and codified in America in the late 1910s then transmitted to other national cinemas through Hollywood's post-First World War exports, eventually becoming the most widely copied film practice. The USSR in the 1920s was one of the foreign film markets that received a heavy dose of Hollywood cinema, for reasons that will be discussed in Chapter 2, providing Pudovkin with considerable exposure to the classical mode and its norms.

Pudovkin proved a quick study, adopting many of its techniques even as he made films that were clearly contributions to the Soviet montage style and thus to the emerging historical–materialist tradition. *The End of St Petersburg* combines elements of each, this despite that fact that those elements might seem to be mutually antithetical. The disjunctive editing of the montage style clearly works against the sequential continuity of the classical mode, for example, and the character-driven actions of classical narration might seem hard to reconcile with a system of supra-individual narrative causality to be found in historical–materialist films.

In appropriating ingredients from both sets of practices, Pudovkin exploited the potential tensions between them. In fact, I will argue that Pudovkin developed a thematic system in *The End of St Petersburg* which explores the dynamic relationship between society and the individual. The two modes allowed him to cover both those dimensions. The historical–materialist mode emphasizes social forces as the source of narrative action; the classical system privileges the individual through the narrative power assigned to its characters. Pudovkin's hybrid film accommodates both, and the interaction of the two styles activates the film's society/individual dynamic.

That Pudovkin attempted to engage both modes in *The End of St Petersburg* speaks to his ambition as an artist. That he succeeded in doing so testifies to his film-making skills. In the following pages, I will try to make evident the source of that ambition and the measure of those skills.

Notes

1. See for example, Noel Burch, 'Film's Institutional Mode of Representation and the Soviet Response', *October*, no. 11 (1979), pp. 77–96.

2. Sergei Eisenstein, *Selected Works, Volume 1: Writings, 1922–34*, ed. and trans. Richard Taylor, London and Bloomington, IN, 1988, p. 144.

3. Vsevolod Pudovkin, *Film Technique and Film Acting*, ed. and trans. Ivor Montagu, New York, 1970, p. 32.

4. An example of the Eisenstein–Pudovkin comparison is to be found in Dwight Macdonald's influential essay 'Eisenstein, Pudovkin and Others', in Lewis Jacobs (ed.), *The Emergence of Film Art*, New York, 1969, pp. 122–46. I will discuss this at greater length in Chapter 4, which deals with the reception of Pudovkin's work.

5. David Bordwell, *Narration in the Fiction Film*, Madison, WI, 1985, esp. chs 9, 11.

6. Ibid., p. 235.

7. Ibid., p. 241.

8. Ibid., p. 235.

9. Ibid., p. 157.

10. On the classical Hollywood cinema and its historical development see David Bordwell, Janet Staiger and Kristin Thompson, *The Classical Hollywood Cinema: Film Style and Mode of Production to 1960*, London, 1985, esp. chs 14–18.

1. Narrative

The End of St Petersburg was made on commission to commemorate the tenth anniversary of the Bolshevik Revolution. As a result, the film's plot focuses on the dramatic events of 1917 and the revolutionary movement centered in the imperial capital of St Petersburg. But Pudovkin also surrounds his depiction of the 1917 Revolution with background material designed to cover events leading up to it. The story time of *The End of St Petersburg* covers a period from 1914 to October 1917, allowing Pudovkin to treat the social situation of Russia on the eve of the First World War, the consequences of Russia's 1914 entry into the war, and the political turmoil of 1917 that finally produced the Bolshevik Revolution.

This historical background would have been familiar to the film's original 1927 audience, either through first-hand experience or through the romanticized version of the Bolshevik Revolution circulated by the Soviet regime. In the manner of historical–materialist films, *The End of St Petersburg* clearly plays on that familiarity, inviting viewers to fill in their knowledge of Russian history in the course of constructing a story logic. Such background information may be less familiar to some readers of this volume, however; so it seems appropriate to account for some of the germane historical incidents in this summary of the film's narrative. Such an account can provide readers a measure of historical context, and it can also suggest how *The End of St Petersburg* actively engages Russia's revolutionary legacy. This account of the film's narrative will thus entail a plot synopsis, as well as a segmentation that distills the highly episodic plot into a recondite form that can be conveniently cited in subsequent analysis. The plot information will then be complemented by a discussion of the historical references that sustain the film's story logic.

Plot Synopsis

The End of St Petersburg opens in rural Russia shortly before the outbreak of the First World War. A montage passage shows landscape shots and images of a village, depicting poverty in the midst of a pastoral setting. The first plot incident centers on the Village Lad and his family. As an older man gives the Lad a meager helping of bread, a pregnant woman staggers to her hut and falls into bed. She gives birth to a daughter, but the infant represents a burden on the family's scarce resources. The Lad must leave the village because his family cannot support another member. Accompanied by an elderly peasant woman, the Lad travels to St Petersburg to seek work.

The film then shifts to a St Petersburg factory, owned by the wealthy capitalist Lebedev, where workers toil under harsh conditions. One worker is identified as a Bolshevik sympathizer (hereafter the Communist Worker), who will emerge as one of the film's central characters. Meanwhile, a factory stockholder visits the foundry. He reprimands a worker over a petty incident and orders him punished. Other workers at the site recognize the injustice of the situation. A montage passage then segues to the city's financial district, where brokers busily engage in stock transactions. The industrialist Lebedev announces that new government arms contracts will enrich his business empire. He manipulates stocks to increase his wealth and gives orders for work to speed up at the factory.

Meanwhile the Lad and the peasant woman arrive in St Petersburg. They walk through the city's streets, searching for the home of an acquaintance from their village who happens to be the Communist Worker introduced in the earlier sequence. They finally arrive at the basement apartment of the Communist Worker and his family. The Communist's wife (hereafter the Wife) is home with her two children, a daughter and a small baby. The Wife greets the new arrivals coldly. She allows them to stay in her sparse apartment but refuses to share food with the hungry travelers. She serves her daughter a modest meal of potatoes and tells the visitors that she can spare them nothing. She explains that trouble is brewing at her husband's factory – an impending strike – and soon her own family will have nothing to eat. There follows an abrupt transition back to the Lebedev factory where workers gather to protest conditions. They confront the factory stockholder (now the factory manager) who tells them they must lengthen the work day to fulfill Lebedev's government contracts. The Communist Worker calls for a work stoppage; this is followed by images of machines shutting down. The strike is under way.

Back at the apartment, the Communist Worker returns home accompanied by several strike organizers. They hold a meeting around the family table while the Wife attends to her baby and the Lad quietly looks on. The Wife complains that the strike will deprive the family of income and leave them all to starve. After the strikers leave, the angry Wife tells the Lad to go out and look for work on his own, because 'nobody is going to feed you'.

The next sequence finds the Lad duly seeking work, and he is recruited as a replacement worker at the Lebedev factory. When strikers confront the scab contingent, police move in to suppress the strikers. The Lad betrays a striker to the authorities and then leads the police back to the workers' tenement. Through the Lad's complicity, the strike organizers are arrested, including the Communist Worker. The Lad receives a pay-off in the form of a coin and work slip, but he is soon remorseful over the betrayal and is berated by the worker's Wife.

The next scene finds the Wife at a shop attempting to purchase provisions for her family.[1] The shopkeeper denies her credit; with her husband in jail, she has no income with which to purchase food. She denounces the merchant and departs the shop, registering growing anger over an unjust system that jails her husband and denies the necessities of life to her children. The Lad then appears at the Wife's flat. He gives her the same coin he had received as a pay-off, perhaps thinking that the gesture would make amends, but she refuses the money. The Lad then goes to the Lebedev office to ask that the Communist Worker be released. His appeal is summarily rejected, and office employees try to throw him out. He fights back, and the scuffle escalates into a small riot that wrecks the office. The Lad is promptly arrested for fighting and hauled off to the district police station, where he is beaten by police and imprisoned without trial.

Later that same night, word comes that Russia has declared war. The event is conveyed through a montage of imperial landmarks around St Petersburg, images of military regalia, expressions of patriotic fervor, and the intertitle motif 'Mother Russia calls!' Meanwhile, the Lad and other prisoners are released from jail and promptly conscripted into the Russian army as 'volunteers' for combat.

The next sequence takes up the war experience through a montage of carnage at the front. Both German and Russian soldiers (including the Lad and the Communist Worker) prepare for an assault. When the battle begins, Pudovkin mixes shots of combat with images of Lebedev and other war profiteers in the St Petersburg financial district. The war drags on for three years, taking the story time to 1917 and the eve of the Russian Revolution. Several images of front-line Russian soldiers enduring hardships also convey their growing dissatisfaction with the war effort and with the regime that put them in the trenches.

That dissatisfaction evolves into revolutionary energy in the subsequent sequence. Shots of munitions production give way to images of Russian women protesting in the streets of St Petersburg over the lack of bread. The Wife is among their ranks and leads a march on a shop to expropriate food. Similar protests sweep across Russia as the uprising of February 1917 takes shape. An intertitle ('Long Live the Provisional Government') confirms that the film has moved forward to the aftermath of the February Revolution. The subsequent sequence offers a caricature of the Provisional Government and its leader Alexander Kerensky. It shows Kerensky receiving applause and adulation from a bourgeois audience whose members are dressed in formal attire. Kerensky tells his admirers that he will bring the war to a victorious conclusion, but his promise is undercut by shots of dead Russian soldiers at the front.

At the Lebedev factory, the Communist worker exhorts his fellow workers to support the Bolsheviks. They join him, and the revolutionary movement gains strength. The plot then shifts back to the Wife alone in her flat at night, awaiting her husband who finally returns from his long absence. He steps out for a moment, and the police soon arrive, hoping to arrest him for subversion. In a daring gesture, the Wife helps her husband escape the police trap.

The next scene takes place in an army camp near St Petersburg where Russian soldiers have been recalled from the front to support the Provisional Government. The Communist Worker arrives at the camp to enlist the soldiers in the Bolshevik cause. He is joined by the Lad, and they lead troops in a mutiny against their officers. This case of rank-and-file rebellion sets the scene for full-scale revolution. An intertitle announces 'Against the Winter Palace', anticipating the assault on the Provisional Government's headquarters in the palace. Red Guard troops attack under a hail of fire and seize the palace. When the assault ends, a title announces: 'St Petersburg is no more.'

The last scene takes place on the morning after the palace attack. The Wife arrives outside the Winter Palace, seeking her husband who was among the assault troops, and she carries a small tin of potatoes. Red Guard fighters, some of whom are wounded, rest outside the palace. The Wife comes upon the Lad among the wounded. She tends to him and shares her potatoes with the soldiers. She then makes her way into the palace and walks through its ornate interior. She finds her husband in the palace, and as the two exchange smiles, a series of titles declare: 'St Petersburg is no more. Long live the "City of Lenin"!' On that celebratory note, the film ends.

Sequence Outline

1. Pre-war period

Sequence 1 – Village Life: Scenes of life in the Lad's village; woman gives birth; Lad must migrate to town to find work.

Sequence 2 – Journey to Town: Lad and old woman travel to St Petersburg.

Sequence 3 – Lebedev Factory: Images of factory work in the Lebedev munitions factory; stockholder punishes a worker over a petty incident.

Sequence 4 – Stock Market: Hectic stock market activity in St Petersburg's financial district; Lebedev manipulates big gains for his company through government arms contracts.

Sequence 5 – Arrival in St Petersburg: Old woman and Lad at St Petersburg train station; they walk through the city, past imperial monuments, on the way to the workers' suburb.

Sequence 6 – Worker's Apartment: The Lad and old woman show up at the flat of the Communist Worker's family; Wife allows them to stay but refuses to feed them; they look on hungrily at a meager meal of potatoes.

Sequence 7 – Strike: Workers confront factory manager at Lebedev plant; Communist Worker leads them in a work stoppage.

Sequence 8 – Meeting in the Worker's Apartment: Communist Worker returns to his flat along with several other workers; they hold a strike committee meeting while the Lad looks on abjectly and the Wife complains about family income lost to the strike.

Sequence 9 – Strikebreakers: Lad joins replacement workers at Lebedev plant; he naively betrays strike leaders, including the Communist Worker; strike organizers arrested; Wife berates the Lad for the betrayal.

Sequence 10 – Confrontation with Merchant: Wife visits shop to acquire food; merchant denies her credit; she denounces him and leaves.

Sequence 11 – Lad and Wife: Lad returns to Wife's flat to make amends; offers her the coin he had received for betraying her husband; she indignantly refuses it.

Sequence 12 – Fight at Lebedev's Office: Lad at Lebedev's office, requests release of the Communist Worker; fights with Lebedev and office employees and is arrested.

Sequence 13 – Police Station: Lad is beaten by police and imprisoned without trial.

2. War period

Sequence 14 – 'Mother Russia Calls!': Russia declares war; patriotic passion sweeps the nation; Lad and other prisoners are released from jail to be conscripted into the Russian army; crowd cheers as Russian soldiers march off to war.

Sequence 15 – Attack: German and Russian troops prepare for battle; the attack begins; battle is intercut with frenzied stock trading in war industries.

Sequence 16 – War Drags On: Soldiers endure hardships in the trenches as the war drags on for three years, into early 1917.

3. 1917 revolutions

Sequence 17 – February Revolution: St Petersburg women, including the Wife, protest bread shortages; they storm a shop to take bread; rebellion spreads through the land.

Sequence 18 – Provisional Government: Kerensky applauded by bourgeoisie; Lebedev vows to control the new regime.

Sequence 19 – Revolutionary Agitation: Communist Worker at Lebedev plant convinces workers to support a proletarian revolution.

Sequence 20 – Husband's Escape: Communist Worker returns home to his Wife; police arrive to arrest him; Wife helps him escape.

Sequence 21 – Mutiny: Russian army units bivouacked outside St Petersburg; Communist Worker and Lad lead soldiers in mutiny against officers.

Sequence 22 – Assault on the Winter Palace: Red Guards prepare for the assault; they attack under fierce gunfire and seize the palace (October Revolution).

Sequence 23 – Morning After: Wife arrives at palace on morning after assault; comforts the Lad and shares potatoes with Red troops; walks through the palace and greets her husband; 'Long Live the "City of Lenin"!'

Story Context

As the above synopsis suggests, *The End of St Petersburg* alludes to recent Russian history and to Soviet interpretations of those historical events. A review of some of that background will help the reader of this study to recoup some of the information that would have been a part of the film's extra-textual system and which would have figured in the original audience's construction of a story logic.

The film's plot breaks down into three general sections, a pre-war interval, the period of the First World War, and the revolutions of 1917. However, Pudovkin generally does not show the political leadership of the era. He does offer a caricature of the Provisional Government's Kerensky (sequence 18), but he does not dwell on the activities or the revolutionary planning of such Bolshevik leaders as Lenin. Instead, Pudovkin's account portrays a revolution from below, through the experiences of a few common, more-or-less anonymous participants. (The central characters are not even assigned proper names in the credits.) The film develops case studies of the experiences of three central characters who constitute something of a cross-section of Russia's working-class population groups: a peasant (the Lad), a worker (the Communist Worker) and an urban woman (the Wife). Each of the three plot sections mixes dramatic scenes depicting the immediate experiences of these class representatives with larger sequences that allude to the historical situation in which they would have lived. The section of the pre-war period outlines day-to-day living conditions for workers and peasants in tsarist Russia; the second section on the World War alludes to the ruinous effect of war on the Russian economy and its further effect on Russian working-class life; and the third section depicts the events of the 1917 revolutions.

The first section (sequences 1–13) provides a sense of daily life in late-imperial Russia by depicting social conditions in both rural (sequence 1) and urban (sequences 3–4 and 6–8) settings. In the opening scene in the village, Pudovkin acknowledges the fact that much of the Russian population lived in rural poverty on the eve of the First World War. The great nineteenth-century industrial revolution that modernized Western Europe by-passed Russia. The vast majority of Russians lived in rural settings throughout the early twentieth century. In 1913, for example, only 13.2 percent of the Russian Empire's population resided in cities.[2] Most of the rest depended on agriculture for their existence. Outmoded farming methods combined with village overpopulation to depress the rural standard of living (sequence 1). There was not sufficient tillable land to support the whole peasant population, resulting in some urban migration (sequences 1–2), although most peasants simply survived in an uncertain rural economy.

The early twentieth century did see a Russian move toward industrialization which was initiated in the 1890s by the tsarist minister Sergei Witte. Annual industrial production increased from roughly 3 billion rubles in 1900 to 5.6 billion in 1913; the factory workforce increased from 2.3 million workers in 1900 to 3.7 million by 1914.[3] This industrial expansion is evoked in the film by the Lad's migration and the ensuing sequences that depict factory life in St Petersburg (sequences 2–3, 5, 7 and 9). That city became the leader of Russian heavy industry (Moscow had more light industries), with large foundries and iron works centered in the Vyborg district.

St Petersburg also contained Russia's most sophisticated financial community. The city's stock exchange, located on the eastern tip of the Vasilevsky Island, became the leading financial center in Russia (sequence 4). Its influence expanded through the 1910s as it capitalized Russia's industrial expansion. This gave rise to a generation of wealthy financier-industrialists – the Putilovs and Vtorovs, for example – who shaped government policy while they funded the growth of Russia's industrial sector.[4] They maintained close ties with the tsarist regime through state contracts for public works and military hardware, and, as is suggested in the film, they sought to influence government policy to their own benefit (sequences 4, 15 and 18).

The character of Lebedev in the film may represent something of a composite of these St Petersburg capitalists, but his enterprise is apparently supposed to suggest the huge industrial empire of Nikolai and Alexei Putilov. With support from the tsarist regime, the Putilovs constructed St Petersburg's (and Russia's) largest factory complex, which produced steel, locomotives and armaments. The Putilovs also controlled a banking network to capitalize their industries. The Putilovs were reviled, however, for their efforts to manipulate tsarist war policy through military contracts and for harsh treatment of their factory workforce; both their war profiteering and their regressive labor practices are alluded to in the film (sequences 3–4, 7, 15 and 18).[5]

Proletarian discontent with working conditions was aggravated by harsh living conditions. Workers and their families had to live in cramped tenement districts in the 1910s. St Petersburg's workers' quarters were hastily and shabbily constructed in response to the recent increase in the worker population, and workers crowded together into spartan tenements. Population density in St Petersburg's worker suburb in the 1910s was twice that of the equivalent working-class areas of Paris, Berlin and Vienna.[6] Scenes in the Wife's austere flat and its surroundings (sequences 6, 8 and 10–11) are designed to convey the difficult day-to-day experiences of that environment.

Whereas much of the film's first section depicts quotidian conditions of lower-class Russia in the 1910s, the situation that fostered discontent and provided the preconditions of revolution, the second section (sequences 14–16) treats Russia's fateful participation in the First World War and the war's effect on Russian society.

War broke out in summer 1914. Russia allied with France and Britain against Austria and Germany, but in the ensuing conflict Russia was left to fight essentially alone on the Eastern Front. Tsar Nicholas II's regime portrayed Russia's war effort as a matter of national pride, and that sentiment quickly took hold within the general population. A great wave of patriotism swept the country immediately after the war declaration, with public demonstrations of support for the tsarist government. Even some anti-monarchist groups rallied behind the government in the name of Russian nationalism. St Petersburg was even given the more Slavic-sounding name of Petrograd as a patriotic gesture. The film invokes the war's start by a montage sequence alluding to that initial war fever (sequence 14).

The situation at the front soon deteriorated, however, as Russia's military proved woefully ill-prepared for extended combat. As military supplies ran low in 1915 and 1916, Russia simply drafted more peasants and workers into the army, eventually putting 14 million men under arms. The scene of the Lad's conscription (sequence 14) provides a distilled dramatization of that process. Those badly-supplied conscripts were often sacrificed to outmoded tactics. Troops were herded into massive assaults in which thousands of men died for little strategic gain. By the end of 1916, Russia had lost a million men killed, 3 million captured, and another 4 million wounded.[7] Such carnage, and the de-humanizing routine of life in the trenches, gradually depressed morale, an effect invoked in the film's wartime episodes (sequences 15–16). Desertion became a problem. More important, Russian soldiers and sailors lost their patriotic spirit and became sympathetic to the revolutionary movement, or at least to any political group that promised to end the fighting. This deteriorating situation set the stage for the revolutions of 1917.

The third section (sequences 17–23) treats those revolutions, covering events from the monarchy's collapse in February 1917 (old-style Russian calendar) through the Bolshevik coup in October. In representing the February Revolution, Pudovkin refers to the street demonstrations of February 1917 that helped bring down the tsarist regime. He shows the women of St Petersburg, including the Wife, protesting food shortages (sequence 17). This is an accurate depiction of the fact that Russian women held mass protests over the wartime food shortages. The demonstrations grew and turned violent, and when tsarist soldiers refused to repress the protesters, joining their ranks instead, the monarchy had clearly lost its power base. Nicholas abdicated on 2 March.

A so-called Provisional Government, composed of left-liberal political leaders, soon assumed authority. They envisioned creating a constitutional governing system, but they never enjoyed enough popular support to rule effectively. They also committed policy blunders ranging from the substantive (keeping Russia involved in the war despite mounting casualties), to the more symbolic (headquartering in the tsars' opulent Winter Palace, a relic of a failed system). Alexander Kerensky eventually assumed the leadership of the Provisional Government, and he determined to lead Russia to victory over Germany (sequence 18). He thus defied growing discontent with the war and pitted the Provisional Government against the resurgent radical parties (including the Bolsheviks) that promised peace. Through the early autumn of 1917, the Bolsheviks maneuvered to gain leadership of the revolutionary movement and to find an opportune time to strike against Kerensky's government, which the Bolsheviks dismissed as a bastion of the bourgeoisie. Pudovkin invokes that view in his comic caricature of Kerensky's regime (sequence 18), but he does not show Lenin's machinations to increase his power base. Instead, Pudovkin provides another grassroots account of growing revolutionary sentiment in 1917, with episodes invoking worker solidarity (sequence 19) and rebelliousness in the ranks of the Russian army (sequence 21). Once again, his depiction of 'revolution from below' privileges the efforts of the common participants more than the Party elite.

This concern with the rank-and-file carries over into the film's dramatic climax, the episode that depicts the storming of the Winter Palace (sequence 22). In fact, the October Revolution was a top-down political action, a coup planned by Lenin and a small coalition of revolutionaries. On 25 October they moved their paramilitary forces into position to control the city, effected the symbolic gesture of seizing the Winter Palace, and maneuvered behind the scenes to wrest control of the radical movement from other leftist parties. The film, however, attends only to the experience of the Red Guards (including the characters of the Lad and the Worker) attacking the palace grounds. In reality, the Winter Palace proved an easy target; palace guards put up little resistance during the assault, and the Provisional Government representatives ensconced inside the palace meekly capitulated. But by 1927, Soviet lore had turned the assault into a heroic struggle, and that romanticized version of the event informs Pudovkin's depiction. His staging suggests a well co-ordinated military assault followed by a bitter but successful fight, but he shows no political vanguard or officer corps running the attack; the Red Guards seem to know how to execute the co-ordinated attack on their own, as an expression of their collective élan rather than the planning of the Party leadership.

That concern with the rank-and-file experience also carries over into the last sequence, as the Red Guards relax at the Winter Palace on the morning after the assault (sequence 23). The scene accurately depicts the calm morning that followed the drama of 25 October in St Petersburg. It also offers a small-scale personal episode, involving the Wife, Worker and Lad, to complement the prior mass scene of the assault. This is in keeping with Pudovkin's strategy of mixing personal stories with larger historical events. The scene contains one historical anachronism worth noting, however. It concludes with the proclamation that 'St Petersburg is no more' and that henceforth the city would be the 'City of Lenin'. By the time of the October Revolution, St Petersburg had already been officially renamed Petrograd. That fact is never mentioned in the film, however, as the city is called St Petersburg throughout, presumably a gesture designed to connect the city with its imperial heritage. (For purposes of consistency, I also refer to the city as St Petersburg in subsequent chapters.) The city would eventually be rechristened Leningrad (Lenin's city), as suggested in the film's finale, but that would not happen until 1924.[8] The second name change was not contemplated in October 1917, as the last scene would have it. That later renaming was, however, an eventual outcome that the film's 1927 Soviet audience members would have known about. The last scene thus plays on their knowledge of that historical outcome and builds that knowledge into the film's conclusion.

Indeed, the narrative of *The End of St Petersburg* consistently plays off such historical knowledge. Its plot centers on the activities of three central characters living through profound historical events. The plot alludes, sometimes cryptically, to those events, activating the audience's prior knowledge of the relevant history. The audience can use that knowledge to construct a fuller story logic. That story logic, in turn, connects the larger historical context to the personal experiences of the film's central characters. This is one of the ways the film balances the general and the specific, connecting individual human experience to the larger operations of history. How and why Pudovkin would endeavor to strike such a balance in the film's design can be suggested, in part, by an account of the film's own historical background.

Notes

1. This scene and the following one of the brief encounter between the Wife and the Lad are missing from most American release and restoration prints of *The End of St Petersburg*. They are in the Library of Congress archival print of the film, however. My thanks to Panayiota Mini for alerting me to

this print discrepancy and for showing the significance of these two scenes to the development of the two central characters.

2. William Blackwell, *The Industrialization of Russia*, Arlington Heights, IL, 1970, p. 44.

3. Ibid., pp. 31–5, 41–5.

4. Ibid., p. 39.

5. W. Bruce Lincoln, *Sunlight at Midnight: St Petersburg and the Rise of Modern Russia*, New York, 2000, pp. 156–8.

6. Ibid., p. 154.

7. Tom Corfe, *Russia's Revolutions*, Cambridge, 1989, p. 26.

8. The naming cycle was finally completed in the early 1990s. With the Soviet system in decay, the city retook its original name of St Petersburg in a gesture of reaction against the communist heritage that survived in the Lenin eponym.

2. Background and Context

While the narrative of *The End of St Petersburg* alludes to the situation of Russia in the years 1914–17, the film as a whole is a product of the Soviet system as it existed a decade later. An interrelated array of historical conditions from the mid-1920s gave shape to the film project that became *The End of St Petersburg*. Those conditions ranged from the evolution of the Soviet Union's leadership to Pudovkin's specific professional situation. This matrix of conditions can account for several issues: why the movie was undertaken in the first place, how and why it took the shape it did, and specifically why Pudovkin combined modes in developing his cinematic account of the Bolshevik Revolution. Hence, this background treatment of *The End of St Petersburg* will not take the form of a chronological narrative detailing the movie's production, although it will include some aspects of the production history. Rather, it will be a layered and sometimes overlapping causal account of the myriad circumstances that shaped this film, detailing the various background conditions that gave form to *The End of St Petersburg*.

Germane to the film's creation are the politics of succession in the Soviet system as the Stalin regime evolved through the mid-1920s, as well as certain policies sustained by that regime. Those policies included the economic system of NEP (New Economic Policy, 1921–28/29), with its mixed economy of Western-style markets and socialist principles of state control. The Soviet film industry took shape within NEP's capitalist/socialist system, and, not coincidentally, Soviet cinema drew its resources and models as much from the market-oriented cinemas of capitalism as from Bolshevik concepts of film propaganda. Pudovkin developed his film aesthetic in this NEP environment of both indigenous and foreign influences, and he worked in the Soviet movie studio that seemed to instantiate NEP's mixed nature, Mezhrabpom. The studio operated as a successful commercial venture, drawing on Western capitalist models, and it also participated in state-sponsored programs of public propaganda with a number of militant revolutionary productions. Not surprisingly, given his professional situation, Pudovkin proved to be as attentive to Western film practices as he was to the montage aesthetic being developed by his Soviet film colleagues. He was in a position to appreciate both, and he drew on both in shaping *The End of St Petersburg*.

As the above synopsis of the film's historical situation suggests, several layers of mediation existed between the general historical conditions of the USSR in the mid-1920s and the movie *The End of St Petersburg*. One can trace out progressively more specific contexts for the film by moving from the situation of the 1920s Soviet leadership, to the NEP system sustained by that leadership, to the Soviet film industry as it emerged under NEP, to the place of the Mezhrabpom studio within that industry, and finally to Pudovkin's circumstances in that studio. The pattern takes one from the general to the specific, and it will reveal a set of symmetrical historical tensions between communist, revolutionary doctrine and the residual influences of Western capitalism, tensions that survived in the mixed system of NEP and which ultimately shaped Pudovkin's views of cinema, finding form in the hybrid design of *The End of St Petersburg*.

NEP and the Bolshevik Party

One proximate cause for Pudovkin's production of *The End of St Petersburg* was the Soviet leadership crisis of 1927. That period marked the tenth anniversary of the Bolshevik Revolution, but it also saw the climax of a power struggle for control within the Communist Party. Those interconnected events would affect many cultural products of the late 1920s, including the nation's feature films.

By the time of Lenin's death in 1924, a leadership rivalry had developed between the ambitious Georgian Joseph Stalin and Leon Trotsky, the brilliant revolutionary theorist. Over the next three years, Stalin maneuvered successfully within Party ranks to consolidate his own power and to weaken possible opponents, most specifically Trotsky. Trotsky and his immediate associates were isolated as a Left Opposition group by 1927. During the tenth anniversary of the Bolshevik Revolution in November, the Trotsky group organized public demonstrations in opposition to the Stalin regime, and the open defiance justified Trotsky's expulsion from the Party. Eventually he was banished from Moscow, and by 1929 he suffered exile from the USSR. Stalin's future as Soviet dictator was assured, although he would continue to eliminate potential rivals through ever more ruthless means, eventually leading to the purges of the 1930s.[1]

The 1927 anniversary was to play a role in Stalin's consolidation of power. The Stalin Party faction saw the anniversary as an opportunity to muster public support through a series of celebrations of the USSR's first decade of existence. The celebrations would contribute to the growing 'cult of Lenin', efforts to deify the dead revolutionary leader and to suggest continuity between Lenin and Stalin, thus justifying the latter's leadership.[2] The anniversary celebrations also marked the new regime's genuine opportunity to take stock of its first decade of existence, a decade in which the Soviets made considerable strides toward modernizing and upgrading the living conditions of a hitherto backward population. The new Soviet leadership declared 1927 a 'Jubilee' year to celebrate both the tenth anniversary of the 1917 Revolution and the advances of the Soviet system in the intervening years. Planning for the anniversary actually began in 1926 and extended through 1927 with a set of commissions for commemorative events and art works. Mass demonstrations and public gatherings were organized to mark various historic episodes of the Revolution, and the arts contributed numerous commemorative plays, paintings, posters, statues, and the like. The Soviet film industry was duly enlisted in the effort through a series of anniversary films.

There was precedent for such commemorative films. The twentieth anniversary of Russia's 1905 rebellion, an uprising characterized by Soviet historians as the prelude to full-scale revolution, had also been marked by anniversary film productions, including two that eventually entered the Soviet film canon: Eisenstein's *The Battleship Potemkin* [Bronenosets Potemkin, 1926], which dramatized the 1905 revolt of sailors in the tsarist Black Sea Fleet, and Pudovkin's own *The Mother*, which took its source from Maxim Gorky's novel about the 1905 uprising.

Several films by leading Soviet directors were commissioned in 1926–27 for the ten-year anniversary. Muscovite director Boris Barnet, fresh from making the successful comedy *The Girl with the Hatbox* [Devushka s korobkoi, 1927], was contracted to direct *Moscow in October* [Moskve v Oktiabre, 1927]. As its title implies, Barnet's film was to treat the role that Moscow played in the October 1917 upheaval, providing something of a counter-balance to the attention normally afforded St Petersburg in most accounts of the October Revolution. Meanwhile, documentary film-maker Esther Shub completed two anniversary projects. Drawing on archival footage, she produced the compilation documentary *The Fall of the Romanov Dynasty* [Padenie dinastii Romanovykh, 1927], an account of Russia under the last tsar and the collapse of the old order. Begun in late 1926, the film was completed in time to mark the tenth anniversary of the February Revolution. She followed that project with a sequel of sorts, *The Great Road* [Velikii put', 1927], timed for the October anniversary. This was also a compilation documentary, drawing from Soviet-era newsreel footage to recount the first decade of the new Soviet system.[3]

Two anniversary projects would receive particular attention, both during their production and in the subsequent annals of Soviet cinema: Eisenstein's *October* and Pudovkin's *The End of St Petersburg*. The two productions would parallel each other in several ways. Eisenstein and Pudovkin were the leading directors of Moscow's two largest movie studios. Eisenstein had won acclaim for *The Battleship Potemkin* and was the star artist of the state-owned Sovkino film studio. Pudovkin had recently earned attention in the Russian film community with *The Mother*, and he was emerging as the A-list director of the privately owned Mezhrabpom film company. Each would receive the prestige assignment of anniversary commissions. *October* was considered important and timely enough for the Sovkino management to summon Eisenstein away from work on a project about Soviet agriculture, and he returned to it only after *October*'s completion, finally releasing the rural feature in 1929 under the title *The Old and the New* [Staroe i novoe]. Mezhrabpom also treated Pudovkin's anniversary film as a high-priority project and offered the director generous financial support and extensive publicity. As we shall see later in this account, the Mezhrabpom studio felt political pressure to support the official anniversary program and to win favor with the new regime.

Such anniversary activities were promoted by the Party leadership out of a short-term motive to consolidate its political power and out of longer-term motives to win support for Bolshevik plans to fundamentally transform the Soviet Union. Trotsky and the Left Opposition were effectively routed after the 1927 anniversary. The Stalin cohort would be free after that to assume full control of the Soviet governing apparatus. They would then move the USSR toward the next phase of its economic development, the accelerated modernization of industry and agriculture under a system of central planning. Stalin and the Party leadership sanctioned a formal Five-Year Plan to guide the Soviet economy from the late 1920s into the 1930s. Beginning in 1928, the Soviet leadership began phasing out the market practices that had been permitted under NEP and moved the Soviet economy to a system of state socialism with official production plans replacing the vestiges of capitalism. Ironically, the Stalin group had supported NEP during the power struggle against the Left Opposition. The Trotsky faction had staked its oppositional identity in part on a critique of NEP, calling for planned economic development. As it happened, central planning was implemented only after the collapse of the Left Opposition. NEP was to endure through 1928 and, in some sectors of the Soviet system, until the early 1930s.[4]

NEP and Soviet Cinema

It was precisely the survival of the NEP system into the late 1920s that actually permitted *The End of St Petersburg* to be made. NEP's market practices permitted the Soviet film industry to grow and even to thrive. And ironically, those market conditions were necessary to provide the resources for Soviet studios to make ambitious communist-inspired films like *October* and *The End of St Petersburg*. NEP's hybrid system created its own contradictions and ironies, as evidenced in the case of *The End of St Petersburg*: a privately-owned studio, pursuing the profit motive in its daily operations, nevertheless welcomed an official charge to make a non-commercial revolutionary film. Such points warrant development, which will come later in this account, but first the NEP system itself needs to be more fully explained.

Although Bolshevik leaders always assumed that only central planning would successfully modernize Russia's economy, exigent circumstances in the early 1920s forced the Bolsheviks to rehabilitate capitalist practices. Russia had endured the privations of both the First World War and civil war with little interruption from 1914 to 1921, and the Bolsheviks had to look to market capitalism to revive a war-torn economy. They also permitted an influential new entrepreneurial middle class to emerge in the same nation that had recently promised to create the first 'dictatorship of the proletariat'. NEP industrial practices borrowed heavily from the capitalist West. The United States, which had achieved the highest level of industrial efficiency of any capitalist nation, provided a handy model for Soviets seeking to introduce modern industrial practices into their own economy. Lenin even advocated studying the theories of the American efficiency expert Frederick Taylor and applying those to the Soviet workplace.[5] Industrial production did indeed increase under NEP, and by 1926 factory productivity eclipsed pre-war outputs.[6] NEP thus nurtured the program of modernization Lenin and his Marxist colleagues had put forth in the name of socialist development, but, during the 1920s, that program went forward through the instruments of Western-style capitalism.

One industry that grew in this market-based economy was film. It is very common to refer to Soviet cinema as a government-owned institution, doing the bidding of the state. Certainly Soviet authorities, through the instrument of the government's Commissariat of Enlightenment, set policy for cinema's development and exerted content control. But the market activities of the film industry under NEP had as much to do with shaping 1920s Soviet cinema as the Soviet regime. Those market conditions account not only for commercial films that circulated in the Soviet distribution market but also for the canonized revolutionary films of the 1920s, including *The End of St Petersburg*; and, as I will try to show, NEP conditions even affected Pudovkin's choices in developing *The End of St Petersburg*.

The fact that Lenin nationalized the Soviet film industry in 1919 is often taken as evidence that cinema functioned as a ward of the state. In fact, his nationalization decree was something of a stop-gap measure to stem the loss of cinema assets at a time when Russia was desperately short of the material resources – cameras, lenses, film stock, projectors – needed to sustain the film industry. The decree would have more significant long-term consequences, however, in that it assured that the Soviet state would have policy-making authority over the film industry. It devolved upon the government's Commissariat of Enlightenment and its energetic head Anatoli Lunacharsky to set film policy guidelines. Thus the state did guide the conduct of affairs for cinema through the 1920s under the mandate of the Lenin decree, especially in the area of film content. Such official production programs as the 1927 anniversary films, including *The End of St Petersburg*, provide examples of the state's intervention into areas of film content. Eventually the state would assume more comprehensive authority for film under the planned economy of the 1930s, but, whatever Bolshevik leaders may have believed about the immediate goals of using cinema as a state instrument for building socialism, they had to look to the NEP market to rehabilitate cinema after the film industry's collapse in the late 1910s. If cinema were ever to have a role as a disseminator of ideology, it first had to function as a viable economic institution.

This was evident early in the NEP era. Lenin authorized Lunacharsky to seek foreign investment if necessary to refurbish the infrastructure of Russian cinema. Overtures went out to the leading cinema capitalists of the West, including Hollywood moguls, to invest directly in rebuilding Russia's extant movie studios; however, with one exception, the foreign

investment initiative failed to garner significant new capital. That exception, as we will see, resulted in the formation of the Mezhrabpom film
company, the studio through which Pudovkin produced *The End of St
Petersburg*.[7]

Foreign trade rather than foreign investment proved the more effective
overall strategy for rebuilding the Soviet cinema. Beginning in 1922 Lenin
and Lunacharsky authorized the importation of masses of foreign films
for commercial release in the Soviet movie market. They correctly calculated that foreign, especially American, movies would appeal to Russian
audiences, including the revitalized NEP middle class, and that the appeal
would produce revenue sufficient to invest in rebuilding the Russian
movie infrastructure. Over the next several years, hundreds of American
and European features entered the Russian market. By the mid-1920s, up
to 85 percent of features playing in Russian movie theaters came from
abroad.[8]

The importation strategy ultimately proved to be economically successful. Revenues from the commercial exploitation of foreign imports,
especially those American movies, played a key role in the industry's
rehabilitation. As a result of the importation policy, the USSR made
impressive annual gains in domestic film output through the 1920s, from
thirteen feature film releases in 1923 to 109 releases just five years later.[9]

Economic progress, though, had to be measured against political
controversy. The decade saw an extended ideological debate – carried
out among cinema personnel, film critics and Communist Party representatives – about the wisdom of importing movies from capitalist nations
at a time when the Soviet cinema was supposed to be promoting the
political goals of communism. Hollywood movies constituted a special
point of concern since they were allegedly suffused in 'bourgeois' and
'counter-revolutionary' ideologies. And the prominence of foreign movies
in the distribution market took audiences away from Soviet-made features
which were expected to contribute to campaigns of mass enlightenment.
Hollywood films often got the longest runs in the prime first-run movie
theaters: even *The Battleship Potemkin* had difficulty competing in commercial release against the likes of Douglas Fairbanks's *Robin Hood*, to
cite one example.[10] The Soviet film industry of the 1920s resided in a
NEP-era contradiction. It needed revenue from foreign films to grow and
even to subsidize the production and distribution of Soviet-made revolutionary films; meanwhile, the imports took away audience members from
those Soviet films and thus undercut the role of Soviet cinema as an
instrument of mass persuasion.[11]

Within the Soviet film community of the 1920s, this problem was often framed as a conflict between commerce and ideology, between pleasing audiences with proven entertainment formulas or educating them with more militant propaganda and montage practices. Leading Soviet film-makers of the decade could not avoid either participating in the debate or having their work framed by it. The likes of Eisenstein, Dovzhenko, Vertov and Pudovkin seemed to constitute a 'left cinema' sensibility (their many aesthetic differences and theoretical disagreements notwithstanding), making revolutionary films in a montage style. But just as important to 1920s Soviet cinema was a group of more commercially oriented Russian directors – Yakov Protazanov and Boris Barnet, for example – whose work seemed to borrow from the audience-tested practices of Hollywood and even from pre-revolutionary Russian cinema.[12]

The ideology versus commerce debate also encouraged some film personnel to consider the possibility of reconciling the apparent conflict between propaganda and popular entertainment. Lunacharsky, for example, who had authorized the Hollywood imports in the first place, argued for an aesthetic synthesis of entertainment and propaganda. Militant films that failed to entertain promised to produce only 'boring agitation', he opined in a 1928 address to film workers; and 'it is well known that boring agitation is counter-agitation.'[13] Soviet directors could, by studying traditional dramas, learn how to make militant films that had broad, popular appeal. Such a synthesis would make a film's ideological message all the more effective for its reach. He advocated the use of devices from popular formulas that promised to engage spectators' interest and emotion – romance, comedy, psychological complexity – and the grafting of those on to militant Soviet films for purposes of audience appeal.

Pudovkin, I submit, would be one of those who consciously borrowed from the American tradition, even as he formulated militant revolutionary messages in his films. He would be identified with the left directors in the 1920s, but he was also sensitive to the popular appeal of American-style entertainment cinema. It was the NEP-mandated presence of those foreign films in the 1920s Russian movie market that created the pre-condition for this aesthetic borrowing by putting Pudovkin into immediate contact with that Hollywood tradition. And the market performance of those Hollywood movies suggested to him their utility as vehicles for mass art. Pudovkin's presence at the Mezhrabpom studio would eventually give him the opportunity to cultivate such interests.

Mezhrabpom and Soviet Cinema

The Mezhrabpom studio often seemed to be trying to maintain a delicate balance between the competing interests of commercial success and political enlightenment that so shaped NEP-era Russian cinema. The company responded to pressures both to entertain and to educate, and the company's young director Pudovkin played a key role in that effort. On the one hand, Mezhrabpom was a product of commercial initiative, and it thrived under the free-market opportunities of the 1920s; but it was also obliged to participate in the official enlightenment campaigns of the 1920s, if for no other reason than to forestall accusations that it was putting profit ahead of public responsibility in its corporate practices.

The company itself was a product of NEP commercialism. It could trace its origins back to pre-revolutionary days, to the tsarist-era film organization Rus, but the economic rebuilding initiative of the 1920s gave rise to the Mezhrabpom company. Specifically, it grew out of Lenin's 1921 invitation to American and European film companies to invest in the fledgling Soviet film industry. That foreign investment offer received only one important taker, and it was not from the ranks of Western capital. The Workers' International Relief (WIR), a leftist organization headquartered in Berlin, had the resources and the sense of mission to help develop Soviet cinema. WIR provided financial assistance to leftist groups in Europe and elsewhere in the 1920s, and it aided the USSR's economic recovery from the privations of war and revolution. WIR used film as one of its fund-raising tactics, making and distributing movies about the USSR. This film background encouraged WIR to invest directly in Soviet cinema to support the Soviet rebuilding effort, and it moved to recapitalize and expand an extant Russian movie company. In 1924 it acquired equity in Rus, renaming it Mezhrabpom, the Russian equivalent of the abbreviation WIR. The German organization eventually took majority control of Mezhrabpom and nurtured its growth through the 1920s.[14]

Mezhrabpom successfully exploited the NEP film market to emerge as one of Russia's two most important film organizations, second only to the state-owned Moscow studio Sovkino. Mezhrabpom's aggressive commercialism accounted for its growth. It specialized in feature productions earmarked for release in major, commercial theaters, films that found favor with Russia's NEP middle class. Mezhrabpom was the first Soviet film company to establish a press bureau to promote new films, and it even purchased three profitable Moscow movie houses as additional sources of revenue. Such commercial acumen paid off in that the company increased its capital from 52,000 rubles in 1924 to nearly 2 million rubles by 1931.[15]

That entrepreneurial energy was certainly necessary as an NEP growth strategy, but it also left the company open to charges of 'nepism', profiteering under NEP. In the commerce versus ideology debate, Mezhrabpom often seemed to be committed to the former at the expense of the latter. The company's production program contributed to this perception, since it stressed genre pictures that were calculated to exploit the entertainment market: e.g. Barnet's comedy *The Girl with the Hatbox*, Protazanov's big-budget science-fiction film *Aelita* [1924] and Konstantin Eggert's popular horror-melodrama *The Bear's Wedding* [Medvezh'ia svad'ba, 1926]. Such programming left the company open to charges that it pandered to a bourgeois audience without contributing to the enlightenment of workers or peasants.[16]

The company acted periodically through the decade to offset such charges with work that appeared to be more public spirited and less concerned with the corporate bottom line. In the middle 1920s, it substantially expanded its program of documentary production, making educational films as loss leaders that enhanced the company's image. And Mezhrabpom included in its production program a quota of didactic, political films calculated to advance the interests of the Soviet regime. For example, the company assigned its veteran director Protazanov to make *His Call* [Ego prizyv, 1925], a melodrama with a strong message of support for the Soviet system. The company could rightly claim that income from its popular commercial films helped underwrite the production of the documentary and revolutionary films that figured in the studio's production plans.[17]

This was the situation when Pudovkin began his film-making career at Mezhrabpom in the mid-1920s. The company was trying to negotiate between profitable practice under NEP and political pressures to contribute educational and ideological films to the presumed benefit of Soviet society. Pudovkin's work would be fundamentally shaped by that tension.

Pudovkin and Mezhrabpom

Pudovkin entered Mezhrabpom in 1925 and soon took part in the company's public-service efforts. It would devolve upon him to make high-profile revolutionary films (e.g. *The Mother*), and he would even contribute to the company's program of educational documentaries (*The Mechanics of the Brain* [Mekhanika golovnogo mozga], 1926). But Pudovkin would also make at least one straightforward entertainment picture, a short comedy that exploited the Russian population's obsession with chess, *Chess Fever* [Shakmatnaia goriachka, 1925]. In other words, he was ready to participate in both dimensions of Mezhrabpom's production program, commercial entertainments as well as ideological and public-service pictures. And in the course of developing his views about film-making, he explored ways to reconcile the two.

He brought to his early film career a set of experiences that would shape that effort. Among them were a background in science and an interest in foreign, especially American, films. Those interests were then refined through his experiences in the early 1920s as a student at the USSR's State Film Institute.

Pudovkin was born 1893 in the provincial town of Penza (a location alluded to in the opening of *The End of St Petersburg*), the son of a salesman. The family relocated to Moscow when Pudovkin was a boy. He eventually entered Moscow University to study physics and chemistry. After military service in the First World War (including time as a prisoner-of-war in Germany), Pudovkin began a career as a chemist in Moscow. He also pursued various artistic interests in his early life, but his intellectual acumen in science, and especially in mathematical practice, would remain with him throughout his life. As we will see, this scientific legacy would resurface in his thinking about film technique.[18]

Pudovkin claimed that he was inspired to shift careers to cinema in 1920 after viewing the American movie *Intolerance* (1916). D. W. Griffith's epic was widely seen in the Soviet Union in the late 1910s and early 1920s, and its complex editing patterns are commonly credited with popularizing the idea of montage with the new generation of Soviet directors. Pudovkin often acknowledged Griffith in general and *Intolerance* in particular as a source for his own views on montage. 'This picture [*Intolerance*] became the symbol of the future of the art of cinema for me,' he asserted.[19]

Also in 1920 Pudovkin encountered the veteran Russian film-maker Vladimir Gardin who had recently been appointed head of the new State Film Institute in Moscow. The institute was established in 1919 to train a new generation of film artists. In this early phase of its history, the small institute could accept practically any interested young person into its student ranks. On the basis of the Gardin meeting and Pudovkin's newly kindled interest in cinema, he was able in 1920 to begin studies as an aspiring film director and actor. He eventually had the good fortune to enter the class supervised by Lev Kuleshov, with whom he studied the theory and practice of cinema.[20]

The Kuleshov Workshop, as it came to be known, was famous for its innovative studies of cinema and for the highly talented circle of students who went on to major careers, including Pudovkin, Barnet and Eisenstein (the latter briefly participated). Shortages of film equipment in the early 1920s meant that the students in the workshop could not make films. Instead they had to learn about cinema through theoretical inquiry into extant film styles. Part of that inquiry involved simply attending commercial cinemas and noting audience responses to various film styles. By this time Moscow's commercial movie theaters were offering mostly foreign movies acquired under the NEP importation program and the lion's share of these were Hollywood features. The Kuleshov group in general and Pudovkin in particular were impressed by the palpable effect American movies had on audiences. The students observed that Hollywood pictures generated more immediate and animated spectator responses than European films did, and they attributed this to the quicker, more sophisticated editing evident in American movies. US imports evidenced far more cuts per minute than did European features, and audiences at those American movies reportedly exhibited proportionately more excitement in response to those editing patterns.

In the light of such findings, Kuleshov spoke admiringly of what he called 'American montage' – his label for the classical Hollywood style – which energized film narratives through editing. In a gesture that harkened up NEP-era admiration of US industrial efficiency, he also complimented the Hollywood style for the efficiency with which it controlled spectator responses. The continuity editing of the Hollywood mode offered the storytelling equivalent of Taylorism, a quick, precise delineation of story information one detail at a time.[21]

Several of the celebrated 'montage experiments' undertaken by Kuleshov and his students – patching together bits of extant film into different combinations and noting audience responses to the edited sequences – actually involved common Hollywood editing practices. The most famous such experiment, for example, revealed the so-called Kuleshov effect, which effect was actually posited on a continuity device. Shots of a neutral face glancing offscreen were intercut with different objects, sometimes reported as a bowl of soup, a corpse and a baby. Subjects viewing the sequence reportedly perceived the face as expressing first hunger, then grief and then joy, a perception that was actually controlled by the three juxtapositions. In fact, the experiment simply investigated an editing pattern widely displayed in the American films then in circulation, the eyeline match. A spectator would, when confronted with an offscreen glance and an object, conclude that the glance fell upon that object. It was a small step to conclude that the glance/object combination revealed the character's psychological state: a face and a bowl of soup combine to evoke hunger.[22]

Pudovkin's experience in the Kuleshov Workshop shaped his later film-making practices in several ways beyond the particular examples cited here; but the importance of Pudovkin's indoctrination in the Hollywood style cannot be overstated. He certainly embraced Kuleshov's 'amerikanshchina' notion that rapid editing energized the film viewing experience and affected spectators, and he along with several Soviet colleagues would refine that insight in the course of developing the montage aesthetic of the 1920s. But just as important for Pudovkin was his exposure to continuity devices deployed in those ubiquitous American movies studied by the workshop participants. Pudovkin eventually tried to apply variants of those devices to his own films, and in so doing he explored how continuity editing could contribute to the didactic film practices of the Soviet Union.

Pudovkin was able to start putting his film training to work in 1925 when he was hired by Mezhrabpom. The studio was in its NEP-inspired growth phase in the mid-1920s, and it expanded its creative staff. Mezhrabpom brought in young talent to complement the old studio hands like Protazanov, and it looked to the Kuleshov Workshop for new directors. Mezhrabpom soon acquired the services of Pudovkin, along with those of his workshop colleague Barnet who became a successful screenwriter and director at Mezhrabpom.

Pudovkin was to make three movies in his first two years at Mezhrabpom before receiving the commission for *The End of St Petersburg*.[23] They constituted a heterogeneous array of production assignments, covering comedy (*Chess Fever*), documentary (*The Mechanics of the Brain*) and revolutionary ideology (*The Mother*). But to some extent, the various components of *The End of St Petersburg*'s mixed style are evident across this array. Taken as a whole, these three earlier works drew on both continuity devices (*Chess Fever*) and more elliptical montage practices (*The Mother*); and they also borrow from both popular conventions (*Chess Fever*, *The Mother*) and principles of public education (*The Mechanics of the Brain*).

Pudovkin began his Mezhrabpom work in spring 1925 by conceiving the project that became *The Mechanics of the Brain*, a documentary about Pavlovian psychology. Pudovkin's scientific background suggested him for the project. He interrupted those plans when he got the opportunity to work on the comedy *Chess Fever*. The project involved a comic turn on the popularity of chess in the USSR, and it thus fit Mezhrabpom's practice of producing crowd-pleasing genre pictures. In fact, *Chess Fever* drew on the fact that the chess master Jose Capablanca, a hero in the

USSR, visited Moscow to participate in a major tournament; Pudovkin worked him into the film to exploit his popularity among Russians.

The film betrays its debt to Hollywood imports. Its physical humor bears a resemblance to American slapstick, especially to the Harold Lloyd films that so captivated Russian audiences. Its editing also harks back to American film practice. Pudovkin clearly used this comic short to explore variants on the continuity devices he had studied with Kuleshov. In the last scene, for example, the movie's heroine, who had previously resisted the appeal of chess, is won over to its pleasures and attends the international chess tournament taking place in Moscow. At the tournament, eyeline matches connect the heroine with her chess-enthusiast beau as well as with several chess masters in attendance. In an application of the Kuleshov effect, Pudovkin intercuts a series of glances with the faces of those several characters. The matched glances and smiling close-ups suggest a sense of the shared pleasures of chess, and that impression is generated through continuity principles.

Pudovkin renewed work on *The Mechanics of the Brain* immediately after shooting *Chess Fever*. In turning to this documentary project, Pudovkin took up more serious material, the science of reflex psychology. If *Chess Fever* represented Mezhrabpom's capacity for entertainment fare, *The Mechanics of the Brain* stemmed from the studio's parallel effort at public enlightenment. *The Mechanics of the Brain* promised to enhance the company's public image and to help offset charges of excess commercialism, and it would help to establish Pudovkin's credentials as a serious filmmaker, one who was able to engage in socially beneficial subject matters.

The Mechanics of the Brain deals with Ivan Pavlov's research into reflex psychology. Pudovkin designed the film to provide technically precise representations of Pavlov's experimental methods. Much of the film is shot and edited in the straightforward, presentational style of educational documentaries. Pavlovian experiments are displayed in shallow sets that offer a clear, simple camera view of the laboratory procedures. A stationary camera then records them in a single take or with only a few functional cuts. Diagrams and intertitles are interspersed with these shots to provide technical explanations of how and why a particular stimulus produces a particular response. There is little in the main body of the film that anticipates Pudovkin's eventual incarnation as either a montage director or a practitioner of continuity editing.

In the last sequences, however, the film takes a turn toward narrative and toward the classical style. The conclusion shows how reflex psychology might offer social benefits. Pudovkin stages scenes of children learning to perform successful group projects through positive reinforcement. The scene is designed to broaden Pavlov's findings on conditioning, to suggest how laboratory knowledge can be translated into effective social behavior. It also humanizes an otherwise dry, pedagogical account of science. The gesture suggests that Pudovkin sought literally to popularize the scientific material by borrowing devices from narrative cinema. He uses the classical plot construction of problem/solution in the small stories of the children trying to overcome obstacles and complete certain tasks. Pudovkin also staged the scenes so as to accommodate classical editing: the children's actions break down into individuated parts through editing, and such continuity devices as 180-degree staging and matches on action tie shots together. Rather as he had done in *Chess Fever*, Pudovkin again explores the utility of the continuity style in *The Mechanics of the Brain*, but this time it was in the service of public enlightenment rather than entertainment.

Pudovkin's effort to work elements of the classical tradition into films designed for public enlightenment culminated with his work on *The Mother*. The film project fitted into Mezhrabpom's effort to earn corporate good-will by participating in state-sponsored public enlightenment campaigns. As noted above, *The Mother* was made on commission to commemorate the twentieth anniversary of the 1905 uprising. Mezhrabpom proposed an adaptation of Gorky's novel about 1905 as a contribution to the anniversary, since that novel was already in the canon of revolutionary literature. Mezhrabpom designated the project as a large-budget, prestige item in its production plans. The adaptation seemed important enough to warrant an extended period of script development and revision. The resulting delays in project development allowed Pudovkin to complete principal photography on *The Mechanics of the Brain* in time to win the commission to direct this major work; he had not been Mezhrabpom's first choice to direct *The Mother*.

The lengthy production schedule also meant that *The Mother* would not be finished until 1926, after the anniversary year. The film was still in preparation when Eisenstein's parallel anniversary film *The Battleship Potemkin* was ready for release. This may have proven fortuitous. It meant that Pudovkin had the model of both that film and Eisenstein's equally experimental 1925 feature *The Strike* available to him while working on *The Mother*. These first two Eisenstein features were certainly profoundly important in establishing the whole Soviet montage aesthetic. For Pudovkin, they provided immediate models that would prove as useful for him as Kuleshov's lessons on classical editing. For the first time in *The Mother*, Pudovkin employed Eisensteinian elliptical montage along with passages of continuity editing.

Pudovkin effected that combination through a spiral-like plot construction in *The Mother*.[24] The film opens on the situation of a nuclear family, a mother, father and son, in 1905 Russia. From that center, the film's narrative spirals out to cover the larger historical events that surround the central characters. The film thus moves from private to public realms of experience, dealing with the personal situations of the central characters and gradually opening up to cover the larger society. It contains both intimate psychological portraits of the central characters, especially the title character, and mass scenes depicting epic, revolutionary events. And Pudovkin employs both continuity practices and Eisensteinian exercises in montage. In scenes such as the opening fight between the father and son and the trial scene, systematic networks of eyeline matches and continuity directional cues evoke Kuleshovian and Hollywood influences; these give way to broader scenes such as the mass demonstration in the film's finale, which evinces a more Eisensteinian design of large-scale action and disjunctive editing.

In combining an emotionally charged account of the title character's personal development with an epic treatment of social upheaval, Pudovkin and his screenwriter Nathan Zarkhi had found a combination that seemed to anticipate Anatoli Lunacharsky's advice that revolutionary propaganda could build on traditional narrative forms which highlight the intimate, psychological experiences of characters. Audiences would, according to this calculation, maintain an emotional identification with a well-developed central character, and that would make the film's ideological message easier to accept. *The Mother*'s positive reception seemed to confirm the wisdom of that strategy. It won favorable reviews and had the best box-office performance of any of Pudovkin's silent features.[25] After this success, Pudovkin would reapply that formula, in a variant, in his next major undertaking, the commission for *The End of St Petersburg*.

Pudovkin and *The End of St Petersburg*

Preliminary work on Pudovkin's anniversary film began in late 1926, and the project evolved substantially over the next several months. Originally the film was to be called *Petersburg–Petrograd–Leningrad* and was to have had a genuinely epic scale.[26] That working title invoked the city's various historical incarnations. St Petersburg drew its original name from its founder Peter the Great, the eighteenth-century tsar who sought to transform Russia into an imperial power. The city's history through the nineteenth century was to be identified with the imperial era of Russian history. With the outbreak of the First World War, the name was changed to the less Germanic-sounding Petrograd, but during the war years the city became the site of intense, revolutionary activity. Finally after Lenin's death, Petrograd was renamed Leningrad to honor Russia's revolutionary leader. The new name carried symbolic weight about the transformation of Russia from an imperialist system to a communist one. The city thus seemed to provide a microcosm of modern Russian history. Its three incarnations offered tidy stages of historical development according to a Marxist model: from imperialism (St Petersburg), through revolution (Petrograd), to communism (Leningrad).[27]

Pudovkin's original conception would have required a broad-based narrative to encompass these three stages of St Petersburg's (and Russia's) historical progress. The story was to spread across the three epochs and measure the social changes in Russia from the imperial era through the early years of the new Soviet regime. This plan for the film would have covered the city's entire history, starting with the 'the building of Petersburg by Peter the Great on the bones of the peasants'.[28] This would have required a highly episodic and elliptical narrative, one that would have sacrificed narrative continuity. This enormously ambitious conception proved impossible to convert into manageable story form, and it would have taxed the resources of Mezhrabpom. Pudovkin and screenwriter Zarkhi scaled down the project. They soon narrowed the focus to cover the city's history from the late-imperial era to the Bolshevik Revolution.

The project thus took on a much narrower temporal range, but the revised script contained a character array that provided an inclusive social cross-section. It called for four intersecting plot lines dealing with figures from various walks of life: an officer-nobleman, the factory owner Lebedev, the Communist Worker and the peasant Lad. These plot lines would have provided case studies of the experiences of every major social class in early twentieth-century Russia. In further revisions of the script, Pudovkin and Zarkhi dropped the character of the officer entirely and diminished the roles to be played by Lebedev and the Worker. As the script moved toward its final revisions, the peasant Lad became the most prominent character. Further trimming eliminated any material dealing with events after the October Revolution. The final script used the storming of the Winter Palace – already a set-piece in Soviet drama – as the movie's penultimate scene and dramatic climax (sequence 22 in the finished film). It was then to be followed by a hastily conceived scene of the morning after the palace attack (sequence 23), which would offer a brief suggestion of the new order to emerge from the Bolshevik Revolution.[29]

The overall effect of these many revisions was to narrow the scope and scale of the movie. The project's first incarnation would have explained the Bolshevik Revolution as the product of grand, epochal stages of historical development. The later, narrower version was designed to present a more limited view of the Revolution through the immediate experiences of a few characters caught up in the events of 1914–17, focusing most closely on only one figure, that of the Lad. The class cross-section would be maintained to some degree in this final draft by the continuing presence of the Worker and the Lebedev character, as well as by the experiences of the Lad, in that the plot would take the Lad through various class incarnations: first as a peasant, then as a worker, then as a soldier and finally as a revolutionary. The revisions sacrificed the epic dimensions of the original conception so as to fashion a story that dealt with specific individuals. Material on surrounding historical conditions would be sacrificed to a drama that offered a more intensified representation of personal experience.

Pudovkin had won praise for using a variant on this strategy in *The Mother*. By concentrating that account of revolution on the title character and her immediate family, Pudovkin achieved a measure of audience engagement through the device of character identification. He broadened the title character's personal story with larger, montage sequences, as we have seen, but the central story of the title character's situation seemed to provide the film with much of its emotional power. Thus, as Pudovkin pared down the scope of the anniversary film, he brought it progressively closer to the model he had employed successfully in *The Mother*. And that model was consciously indebted to the classical Hollywood system of narration, the same classical system that had already established a solid track record with Soviet audiences thanks to those American imports.

By the time he was involved in script development of *The End of St Petersburg*, Pudovkin had recently finished writing a set of theoretical tracts that offer insight into his views about the utility of that classical Hollywood model.[30] Hollywood's character-centered plots and practices of continuity editing make for clear, precise narratives that promised to engage spectator attention and sympathy, Pudovkin believed. On such sturdy narrational vehicles effective propaganda could be mounted. In particular, continuity editing seemed to guide a spectator's attention from one detail to the next. It could break down information into small units as individual shots and organize them in tidy, linear fashion. The spectator could then take in the information as a sequence of small, unambiguous details, with the continuity devices tying those details together into an equally unambiguous sequential logic. Effective continuity editing seemed to Pudovkin to eliminate the 'confusion by linkage and wastage by intervals [that] are inevitable attributes of nature'.[31] The system worked with almost mathematical precision, Pudovkin suggested, and he evoked mathematical analogies to explain the communicative efficiency of classical editing (recall Pudovkin's background in science). A cinema that hoped to convey messages of political enlightenment to spectators could draw on the conventions of continuity to assure the effective transmission of those messages.

When Pudovkin was revising the conception of *The End of St Petersburg* in 1927, scaling down its early excesses, these views about the classical mode clearly shaped his creative decisions. They had been formulated over the course of his early career at Mezhrabpom, through his exposure to imported movies in the NEP film market and through his association with another Hollywood admirer, Kuleshov. They also informed the script revisions that pushed *The End of St Petersburg* toward the tighter, character-centered narrative model of the classical system.

That model was not the only one that shaped *The End of St Petersburg*, though. Indeed, had Pudovkin simply told his story of revolution through strict, unswerving allegiance to the classical paradigm, he would have been confronted with a vexing ideological problem: how does one account for larger historical events that cannot be explained through the actions and motives of individual human agents? The classical mode often involves characters with stated ambitions whose actions are calculated to achieve those ambitions. Those actions, in turn, motivate narrative events. In the classical narrative, events are thus caused by the goals and actions of individual human beings.[32] This narrational model would seem to be at odds with Marxist explanations of history which privilege impersonal forces and which inform the historical–materialist mode of narration. Marxist political theory – and Soviet doctrines deriving therefrom – might explain historical events through such broad causes as class conflicts or shifts in relations of production. Dialectical social forces rather than personal ambitions might be necessary to explain something as complex as a political revolution. For Pudovkin, whose task it was in *The End of St Petersburg* to depict just such a revolution, there remained the problem of how to account for such historical dynamics. Whatever his allegiance to classical Hollywood, he would have to appeal to an alternative narrational strategy to depict revolution as something more than the doings of a few characters.

Such models were, of course, being developed by Pudovkin's contemporaries in the Soviet avant-garde. The most proximate and most important of these for Pudovkin was clearly his friend and occasional rival Eisenstein. Certainly Eisenstein employed experimental film designs in his early features *The Strike* and *The Battleship Potemkin*. As is well known, those films employed mass heroes in lieu of conventional protagonists, and dialectical rather than linear narrative forms. As we have already seen, Eisenstein's early montage experiments in those films influenced *The Mother*, an aesthetic debt that Pudovkin was happy to acknowledge.[33]

Fortuitous circumstances put Pudovkin and Eisenstein in close contact in 1927 while both were working on their respective anniversary films and those circumstances helped produce a salutary cross-fertilization. The two artists were literally brought into immediate creative proximity by their parallel assignments of making films on the October Revolution. Both did location shooting in Leningrad in overlapping production schedules in 1927. They even took turns filming in the locales that had witnessed the original revolutionary events of 1917. 'I bombarded the Winter Palace from the *Aurora* while Eisenstein bombarded it from the Fortress of St Peter and Paul,' Pudovkin later claimed, in a colorful though perhaps hyperbolized anecdote. 'One night I knocked away part of the balustrading of the roof, and I was scared I might get into trouble, but luckily enough, that same night Sergei Mikhailovich [Eisenstein] broke 200 windows in private bedrooms.'[34] The two directors were in something of a race to complete their productions by 7 November, the precise anniversary date. By scaling down his project along lines already discussed, Pudovkin met his deadline. Eisenstein's *October* came in late, in part because Eisenstein apparently had to make some last-minute revisions to reduce Trotsky's role in the film – fallout from the Stalin–Trotsky power struggle. Since Pudovkin's narrative did not refer to the Party leadership (see Chapter 1), he suffered no such revisionist problems.

Even as a work-in-progress, Eisenstein's *October* influenced Pudovkin's evolving conception of *The End of St Petersburg*, apparently as a result of the two artists' creative proximity. While still working on his film, Pudovkin was able to see edited sequences from *October*, and he later acknowledged his admiration for the montage practices evidenced therein. Pudovkin especially admired those sequences in *October* in which the editing defied conventional time and space. Kerensky's climb up the Winter Palace's Jordan Staircase, for example, departs from a realistic depiction of the character's ascent to make a rhetorical point about Kerensky's political rise to power. Eisenstein's montage in such moments depicts not just an individual's action, but the larger meaning of such action.[35]

Such sequences were Eisenstein's early montage experiments in a style that he would label 'intellectual montage'.[36] Eisenstein conceived this as editing that would not so much depict narrative action as advance fuller intellectual examinations of historical events. These would be designed to enhance the spectator's understanding of history via Marxist analysis. Passages in *October* put this new notion of montage to the test. Such passages drew from a broad array of images that are held together by a common ideological motif rather than conventional narrative continuity. For example, in fashioning the 'God and Country' sequence of *October*, Eisenstein departed from the narrative of the 1917 Revolution to juxtapose an assortment of religious icons. The passage was designed to reflect on the politically reactionary effects of religion. Thus Eisenstein could balance dramatic re-creations of the revolutionary events of 1917 with intellectual montage passages that explore the larger implications of those events. As employed by Eisenstein, intellectual montage suggested a means to deal with supra-individual historical causes, in this case, the influence of religion.

Eisenstein's timely influence may have helped Pudovkin solve the problem of how to represent impersonal historical forces in *The End of St Petersburg*. Pudovkin applied his own variant of intellectual montage in several passages of the finished film. In a manner not so very different from Eisenstein, Pudovkin developed wide-ranging, open-ended montage passages to explore abstract concepts such as patriotism: e.g. the montage sequence beginning with the title 'Mother Russia calls!' (sequence 14). Such passages seem designed to help establish the larger social context for the specific experiences of the film's central characters. Pudovkin's application of intellectual montage was also calculated to effect a system of narrative causation separate from the classical model of character motivation. Pudovkin opted to use montage to illustrate those supra-individual forces that were not normally accounted for in the Hollywood paradigm, but which, according to Soviet doctrine, were fundamental to the historical process.

Through timely applications of intellectual montage, Pudovkin was able to develop broad political themes on poverty, industrial relations, imperialism and war. Those were to be counter-balanced with more intimate scenes depicting the specific experiences of a few central characters, the latter shot in a continuity style indebted to the character-based narratives of the Hollywood paradigm. The classical model offered the virtues of narrative economy, precision and audience engagement; Eisensteinian montage promised the possibility of grand scope, aesthetic dynamism and an explanation of historical processes that could be reconciled with Marxist doctrine. Pudovkin applied both styles in complementary measures in *The End of St Petersburg*.

Whereas in *The Mother* Pudovkin began the film as a family chronicle and gradually expanded the film's narrative boundaries to engage a larger historical scope, in *The End of St Petersburg* he chose to move back and forth between the two modes of intellectual montage and classical continuity. This permitted Pudovkin to develop two parallel lines with complementary narrational scales: small case studies of individual human beings caught up in a revolution, as well as larger explorations of the historical conditions that produce such revolutions.

In the course of downsizing his anniversary film from the grandiose *Petersburg–Petrograd–Leningrad* to the more character-centered *The End of St Petersburg*, Pudovkin sacrificed epic scale. He hoped to compensate with a narrative that offered the benefits of audience identification. But the application of Eisensteinian montage to *The End of St Petersburg* gave him the opportunity to open the narrative up again – to extend its narrational horizons – and to find a narrative scale commensurate with the epic dimensions of a historic revolution.

One might be tempted to conclude that Pudovkin's hybrid design was simply a compromise between the alternative aesthetic practices of two respected colleagues, between Kuleshovian continuity and Eisensteinian montage. In fact, Pudovkin was responding to a complex matrix of determinations that took shape in the 1920s, the delineation of which has been the purpose of this background account. The politics of the 1927 anniversary led to the production of *The End of St Petersburg* in the first place, of course; but this also had the consequence of bringing Pudovkin and Eisenstein together in parallel projects that would produce a beneficial cross-over influence. More fundamentally, the NEP system shaped Soviet cinema in ways that would directly affect Pudovkin and *The End of St Petersburg*. The NEP-era Soviet film industry put Pudovkin in contact with the classical Hollywood style, via those American imports, at the formative moment of his film career. In the course of studying with Kuleshov and developing his own theories, Pudovkin had the chance to refine his familiarity with the classical style, especially how and why the style seemed to affect audiences. Then in his working situation at Mezhrabpom – the studio that exemplified the conflict between NEP commercialism and Soviet mandates of public enlightenment – Pudovkin had to find ways to reconcile the Hollywood tradition with the mission of making *engagé* political films. His timely borrowing from his Soviet film colleagues allowed him to do that. The result was the composite form of *The End of St Petersburg*.

Notes

1. These events are described in any number of sources on Soviet political history. For a tidy summary of Stalin's political ascent, see Alan Wood, *Stalin and Stalinism*, London and New York, 1990, chs 3–4.

2. On the Lenin cult and its formation, see Nina Tumarkin, *Lenin Lives! The Lenin Cult in Soviet Russia*, Cambridge, MA, 1983.

3. Jay Leyda, *Kino: A History of the Russian and Soviet Film* (3rd edn), Princeton, NJ, 1983, pp. 222–6.

4. Alec Nove, *An Economic History of the USSR, 1917–1991* (3rd edn), London, 1992, ch. 6.

5. Louis Fischer, *The Life of Lenin*, New York, 1964, pp. 258, 605.

6. Nove, *Economic History*, p. 89.

7. I. N. Vladimirtseva and A. M. Sandler, *Istoriia sovetskogo kino, 1917–1967*, 4 vols, Moscow, 1969–76, Vol. 1, p. 30; I. S. Smirnova (ed.), *Samoe vazhnoe iz vsekh iskusstv: Lenin o kino*, Moscow, 1973, pp. 105–7, 169–70.

8. Betty and Vance Kepley, 'Foreign Films on Soviet Screens, 1922–1931', *Quarterly Review of Film Studies*, 4, no. 4 (1979), p. 431.

9. Richard Taylor and Ian Christie (eds), *The Film Factory: Russian and Soviet Cinema in Documents, 1896–1939*, Cambridge, MA, 1988, p. 424.

10. See Richard Taylor, *'The Battleship Potemkin': The KINOfiles Film Companion*, London and New York, 2000, pp. 65–76.

11. See Denise Youngblood's excellent account of the dilemma of importing films and foreign ideologies at a time when Soviet cinema was supposed to be promoting a program of mass persuasion: *Movies for the Masses: Popular Cinema and Soviet Society in the 1920s*, Cambridge, MA, 1992, esp. chs 2–3.

12. Ibid., chs 6–7.

13. Lunacharsky, 'Speech to Film Workers', in Taylor and Christie (eds), *Film Factory*, p. 197.

14. Iu. A. L'vunin, 'Organizatsiia Mezhdunarodnaia Rabochaia Pomoshch' i sovetskoe kino', *Vestnik Moskovskogo Universiteta*, 9, no. 4 (1971), pp. 21–8.

15. Ibid., pp. 28–33. Willi Münzenberg, *Solidarität: Zehn Jahre Internationale Arbeiterhilfe 1921–1931*, Berlin, 1931, pp. 511–17, 520.

16. Youngbood, *Masses*, pp. 84–6, 110, 115–16.

17. L'vunin, 'Organizatsiia', pp. 28–30.

18. A. Mar'iamov, *Vsevolod Pudovkin*, Moscow, 1951, pp. 14–15; A. Karaganov, *Vsevolod Pudovkin*, Moscow, 1983, pp. 3–5.

19. Quoted in Leyda, *Kino*, p. 150.

20. Karaganov, *Pudovkin*, pp. 5–8.

21. Lev Kuleshov, *Kuleshov on Film*, ed. and trans. Ronald Levaco, Berkeley, CA, 1974, pp. 45–51.

22. On these experiments and their place in the activities of the Kuleshov Workshop, see Vance Kepley, 'The Kuleshov Workshop', *Iris*, 4, no. 1 (1986), pp. 19–21. See also the fascinating dossier in *Film History*, 8, no. 3 (1996),

pp. 357–67, which re-creates certain of the Kuleshov experiments from surviving fragments and first-hand accounts.

23. On Pudovkin's early career at Mezhrabpom, see Karaganov, *Pudovkin*, pp. 20–6.

24. This concept is from Panayiota Mini, 'Pudovkin's Cinema of the 1920s', PhD dissertation, University of Wisconsin-Madison, 2002, ch. 4.

25. L'vunin, 'Organizatsiia', p. 33, n. 90. *The Mother* was selected as one of the ten favorite feature films in a 1927 movie audience poll (A. I. Troianovskii and R. I. Egiazarov, *Izuchenie kino-zritelia*, Moscow, 1927, p. 31).

26. Karaganov, *Pudovkin*, p. 82.

27. See Katerina Clark's *Petersburg: Crucible of Cultural Revolution*, Cambridge, MA, 1995, for a rich account of the myriad cultural associations that attach to the city of St Petersburg. The city's history is recounted in W. Bruce Lincoln, *Sunlight at Midnight: St Petersburg and the Rise of Modern Russia*, New York, 2000.

28. Pudovkin, 'Pudovkin on His Early Films', in Peter Dart (ed. and trans.), *Pudovkin's Films and Film Theory*, New York, 1974, p. 63.

29. Ibid., pp. 63–5.

30. The theoretical tracts took the form of two monographs on film-making. They were completed in late 1926, between the release of *The Mother* and the early script development of *The End of St Petersburg*. These writings form the core of the English-language volume of Pudovkin's theory, *Film Technique and Film Acting*, ed. and trans. Ivor Montagu, New York, 1970.

31. Ibid., p. 93.

32. See David Bordwell, *Narration in the Fiction Film*, Madison, WI, 1985, ch. 9.

33. Dart, *Pudovkin's Films*, pp. 61–2.

34. Quoted in Leyda, *Kino*, p. 235.

35. V. Pudovkin, 'S. M. Eisenstein (From *Potemkin* to *October*)', in Taylor and Christie (eds), *Film Factory*, pp. 199–200.

36. Eisenstein advanced the concept of intellectual cinema in 'Perspectives', *Selected Works, Volume 1: Writings, 1922–34*, ed. and trans. Richard Taylor, London and Bloomington, IN, 1988, pp. 151–60. For an account of its application in *October*, see Noel Carroll, 'For God and Country', *Artforum*, 11, no. 5 (1973), pp. 61–5.

3. Analysis

Pudovkin's commission to commemorate the Bolshevik Revolution bore the assumption that his film would support the Bolshevik regime by celebrating the Revolution's outcome. But, as noted previously, *The End of St Petersburg* omits the Bolshevik hierarchy. Whereas Eisenstein's parallel anniversary film *October* focused on Party leadership and planning, down to the minute-by-minute scripting of the 25 October coup, Pudovkin's account takes up the role of those common participants whose names would never enter the Bolshevik pantheon. And alterations during script development scaled the project down so as to focus on the small stories of a few fictional protagonists, balancing them against background material on Russian history. The consequence of Pudovkin's revisions was to put forth an account of revolution that explored the contribution of rank-and-file participants, thus setting his project off somewhat from the many Leninist panegyrics routinely propagated by the Soviet regime.

More generally, Pudovkin's film treats the participation of common people in major historical events. It explores the conditions that make seemingly powerless, unremarkable individuals into agents of historical change. He does so by the mix of narrative scales and styles addressed in the last chapter. This will be the central concern of the ensuing analysis. Through an exegesis of the film's narrative design and its style, I will explore Pudovkin's rendering of the role of the private citizen in political action, and I will argue that in *The End of St Petersburg*, Pudovkin puts forth a view of revolution that stresses personal empowerment. His account suggests that the Soviet Revolution enhanced the power of private citizens. Its social benefit was not just the triumph of the proletariat as a class, but the political habilitation of that class's individual members.

That theme of empowerment develops gradually through the length of the narrative. In the early episodes of *The End of St Petersburg*, the main characters are represented as victims of conditions they cannot control. They then gradually develop political awareness through the course of the film. As a result, they emerge as participants in political actions in later scenes, proactive agents of change rather than passive victims of historical conditions. The film's conclusion then portrays them as victors, strengthened by the very revolution they helped bring about.

That evolving power relationship is measured through the narrative roles played by the three central characters. The Lad serves as the film's main character, with two other figures, the Wife and the Communist Worker, present as complements against which one can measure the Lad's evolution. The Lad has the most narrative prominence in the film. He figures in fourteen of the film's twenty-three sequences (the Communist appears in ten sequences, the Wife in eight). And the Lad goes through the most extensive character development. He passes through several class identities in the course of the film: from peasant, to worker, to soldier, and finally to revolutionary. Indeed, the film takes him through a microcosmic version of Russia's late-imperial history, as he experiences the historical events of industrialization, war and finally, revolution. His progression is prompted by those shifting class identities as he moves from being a passive figure, the pawn of a repressive social system (sequences 1, 2), to an active one, a revolutionary who helps effect historical change (sequences 21, 22).

The character of the Wife complements that of the Lad, exemplifying the experience of Russian women in the same historical setting. Her experiences parallel the Lad's in many ways, she in the domestic sphere (family life) and he in the public sphere (production). Whereas he is identified with production by working in agriculture (sequence 1) and industry (sequence 2), she is identified with consumption, the food for her family. We see her feeding her children (sequence 6) or attempting to secure provisions for her family (sequence 10). Like the Lad, she also gradually acquires political consciousness and becomes politically active. And consistent with her identity as a provider, her progress is measured through the food motif in that she participates in the bread riots of February 1917 (sequence 17) and even shares potatoes with Red Guards in the last scene (sequence 23).

Her Communist Worker husband is present to provide a model of enlightenment that other characters can follow. Unlike the other main characters, he does not gradually acquire political consciousness. Rather he has that trait *a priori*. When he is first shown in the film, an intertitle identifies him as a 'Bolshevik' (in some prints he is a 'Communist organizer'), and he is able to advise other workers on proper political action from the start (sequence 3). He then serves as the instigator in each major move the masses take toward proletarian uprising, including the strikes (sequences 7, 8, 19) and the army mutiny (sequence 21). His Bolshevik affiliation does bring the Communist Party into the film via his proxy. But it is worth restating that the Party elite is not represented. This particular Bolshevik is a rank-and-file figure, a common worker who apparently learned to grasp the benefits of Marxism on his own, not a Party intellectual or full-time revolutionary like Lenin. He is something of a *primus inter pares* (first among equals) figure with respect to other workers. He leads by example, stepping forward out of a group of workers at decisive moments to inspire others to take action (e.g. the strike in sequence 7).

The Communist's relative stability as a character type – an enlightened worker who translates his knowledge into timely action – is in contrast to the fuller character shifts of the Wife and Lad. The Communist's thematic function is to provide a form of political sophistication; his enlightenment is present throughout the film and available for the Wife and the Lad to emulate. In this respect, *The End of St Petersburg* employs a narrative model common to Soviet fiction, involving a mentor–disciple relationship. A character who is already politically sophisticated guides a more naive character or characters down the road toward revolutionary consciousness. The narrative stresses the revolutionary development of the disciple, who emerges from common origins and eventually becomes a committed communist. Such a development is built on the mentor's prior awareness of communism's benefits, and that development, in turn, provides a model for audience members to imitate: if a typical peasant (the Lad) or a typical urban woman (the Wife) can eventually become a believer in and beneficiary of communism, then so, rhetorically, can any member of the audience. As Katerina Clark has shown, such mentoring tales became a proven formula of the Soviet didactic novel. They proved readily adaptable to didactic films, and Pudovkin did so. One of the prototype texts for this formula was Gorky's novel *The Mother*, in which a young revolutionary sets a positive example for the title character, his own mother.[1] Pudovkin's film adaptation of the novel retained that formula. He reprised it in *The End of St Petersburg*, even recasting the title-role actress from *The Mother*, the brilliant Vera Baranovskaia, in the role of the Wife.

The pattern of personal development emerges in stages through the course of *The End of St Petersburg*'s three major sections, and it is sustained through Pudovkin's practice of shifting between the small-scale sub-plots of his three major characters and larger accounts of their historical situations. The narrative takes on a highly episodic quality because of the frequent shifts back and forth among the plotlines, but a network of motifs having to do with the characters' parallel evolutions helps tie the episodes together into a coherent account of personal habilitation.

I. Pre-war Period

The first section (sequences 1–13) treats Russia's late-imperial period in the months before the First World War and evokes Russian daily life before it was interrupted by war. There is little sense of forward movement of historical time in the opening, no dates or historical markers to indicate exactly when things are happening. Such historical indicators begin with the declaration of war in the second section, and only then does the film's story time take on a palpable forward momentum.[2] The opening offers more of a synchronic sense of life in tsarist Russia, with typical day-to-day experiences of various population groups: e.g. farming (sequence 1), factory life (sequence 3), family life (sequences 1, 6). The leisurely sense of story time in the opening section contrasts with the more accelerated rate of change shown in sections II and III as the momentum of revolution builds, a shift designed to suggest that a desultory society would be energized by the revolutionary movement. The one major historical trend the first section does invoke is Russia's early twentieth-century industrialization effort and the attendant decline of the agricultural sector. This motivates the Lad's move from one sector of society (peasantry) to another (proletariat). More significantly, it is set up as a large-scale economic problem, a structural condition of pre-revolutionary society, which is beyond the control of the central characters but which nevertheless affects their lives.

Sequence 1: Village Life

The opening sequence at the village establishes this relationship between economics and the individual. The first montage sequence even makes a connection between the rural environment and the peasants, between the land which is the source of the agricultural economy and the people who participate in that economy. The film opens with a rural landscape shot, two shots of windmills, a field with haystacks, and then a close shot of an elderly peasant man eating bread. The shot sequence also contains an intertitle that alludes to the people of the Penza, Novgorod and Tver regions. That expository title generalizes, suggesting that one could apply this scene to other Russian regions, as though the poverty and humble existence visible in this village could apply anywhere in tsarist Russia. Furthermore, the image sequence treats the various relationships of the agricultural economy in a brief application of intellectual montage: the land, rudimentary technology (windmill), signs of peasant labor (haystacks) and the product of that labor (bread) are included in the image array. The montage links those elements as the basic ingredients of the tsarist-era agricultural system and as the economic context for the peasants' lives.

Sequence 1 also provides the film's first plot event, the birth of a child. The style shifts toward continuity to depict the incident. In a set of continuity cuts, a pregnant woman moves to a hut, enters and begins labor. Meanwhile, the Lad and the elderly peasant share bread in an exterior setting. Conventional cross-cutting links the two spaces and confirms the two events' simultaneity. Thus from the opening montage that generalizes about Russian agriculture, the film moves quickly to a particular peasant family and a particular experience, the birth of a child. It moves from a broad montage to a tighter continuity passage in the process. And it connects the fate of that family to conditions obtaining in the larger agricultural setting.

That becomes apparent when the family's existence is disrupted. As the scene plays out, we learn about the effect of overpopulation in the agricultural sector. The Lad plows the field as the older man returns to the hut to find that his wife has given birth to a daughter. Pudovkin uses a variant of continuity editing in the scene inside the hut, with character glances to register the sense of the moment. The father's glance is connected to the newborn baby through a version of the Kuleshov effect. But in this instance, the effect does not connote joy (recall the face-and-baby-equal-joy Kuleshov experiment). The father's visage registers a troubled response, and the scene plays against the expectation of celebration that might normally accompany childbirth. In this sequence, the child is portrayed as burdensome, an additional obligation for an impoverished family.

At this point, it is worth noting that Pudovkin's application of continuity editing often involves a variant of Hollywood practice rather than a slavish adaptation of the norm. He usually does not open a scene with a wide-scene establishing shot followed by medium and close shots that break the space down; such would be the most familiar way of articulating the space of a scene under the classical model. Pudovkin usually eschews the establishing shot and builds a space up from smaller details, using glances and matches on action to connect spaces. He often positions a character in a setting, and then has that character glance here and there at the surrounding spaces. The angles of the glances provide an impression of spatial cohesion from one shot to the next (even though the scene may include cheat cuts). The glances and reaction shots activate the Kuleshov effect, signaling the character's response to what he/she sees. This application of continuity concentrates the audience's attention on that character's situation and on his/her reaction to that situation. As we will see, Pudovkin uses this pattern several times in the film in the intimate scenes involving his main characters. It thus figures in his strategy of developing small stories which highlight specific character experiences and which work in contrast to the open-ended montage sequences which lack a point-of-view character.

In the first application of continuity, the childbirth scene, the style functions to highlight the characters' reaction to the birth. The scene in the hut matches the glances of the father, mother and midwives around the central fact of the baby. The glances do not provide consistent screen direction, but the absence of an establishing shot helps hide any incon-sistency in the characters' locations. What is important is the character psychology registered in the reaction shots, and that is an apparent tension over the presence of this baby.

The next passage opens up the space of the sequence and explains the source of that tension. Through cross-cutting, we see the Lad plowing a field while the old peasant and mother inside the hut continue to con-template the child's arrival. Two intertitles declare that there will be an 'additional mouth to feed' and 'one more new proletarian'. Those titles bracket shots of the figures inside the hut looking at the baby, shots of the infant, and shots of the Lad plowing a field. This montage combina-tion suggests a family that has grown beyond the size allowed in the zero-sum game of Russia's depressed agricultural economy; an addition to the family requires an equivalent subtraction from the family. The reference to the 'new proletarian' is juxtaposed with shots of the Lad plowing the field. This association shows him working the land even while it identifies him with industry, a purposeful irony that comments on the decline of the peasant community.

Sequence 2: Journey to Town

The journey montage contains another disjunction, this time between the two halves of the overall sequence. The first half involves the journey of the Lad and an older peasant woman through the countryside to the city, and the second half shows their destination, St Petersburg. Both the pacing and the *mise-en-scène* patterns of the two halves create a contrast

Figure 1

between rural and urban environments, and they set up the idea that St Petersburg will prove to be an alien environment for the protagonist.

During the journey, the rural landscape appears open and uncluttered. The two travelers are framed so as to offer wide views of the empty space around them (Figure 1). They seem to move through an open, boundless environment, an evocation of Russia's vast rural terrain. Low contrast, monochromatic imagery gives a dull, gray quality to the environment, and the shots have an even distribution of light. The editing has a leisurely pace (an average shot length of 7 seconds); the characters move slowly, an effect that is reinforced by overcranked shots of them walking along the road. And point-of-view shots of the characters' journey show the surrounding terrain moving gracefully past their line of vision. These elements combine to indicate the considerable length of the journey, the distance between village life and city life, as it were. But it also reminds the viewer of the open, unfettered experience possible in the rural setting.

This contrasts with the urban environment the characters enter in the latter half of the episode. A title identifies the new setting as St Petersburg, and it is followed by shots that are starkly different from the rural *mise-en-scène*. The montage offers no overview of the city, but rather a series of statues and buildings that constitute city landmarks. As opposed to the open spaces in the previous montage, St Petersburg's *mise-en-scène* seems crowded with the solid objects that make up a city setting, and Pudovkin's cinematographer Anatoli Golovnia shifts to a higher-contrast black and white to depict dark, heavy shapes and refracted areas of light. The objects tend to loom up over the camera, blocking out light and disrupting any possible sense of open space. They seem to rise up to fill the frame. The main camera position was from above on the rural road but from below in the city. For example, the Bronze Horseman, the city's most familiar statue, is shot from oblique, lower angles. The whole statue is not shown, only parts of the horse and rider appear on screen with other parts falling outside the frame (Figure 2). Certain landmarks appear as reflections off water surfaces; the palace district along the Neva River is literally refracted by the river's presence. The quivering surface of the water alters the appearance of the imperial buildings themselves, as Amy Sargeant has noted, a portent of the old order's instability.[3]

Such cryptic representations of St Petersburg defamiliarize an environment that would have been familiar to Pudovkin's original audience. The signs of the tsarist heritage, preserved in the city's architecture and monuments, appear as strange and distant objects. The representations evoke the sense of abstraction experienced by the newly arrived peasant Lad. While not part of formal point-of-view set-ups, such shots might suggest the experience of a stranger, wandering the streets of the city,

Figure 2

looking up at these statues for the first time. The city's great monuments seem distant yet powerful in this initial encounter, setting up a pattern that will be addressed later in this analysis, wherein such imperialist icons will gradually be brought down to a more human scale in the film's later episodes as a measure of the central characters' increased sense of strength.

Sequence 3: Lebedev Factory

The cityscape montage segues into a montage of factory life, and the contrast with the rural environment continues. Miscellaneous images of factory settings, with billowing smoke, begin the sequence, followed by shots of workers in a munitions plant. The sequence uses a stark, high-contrast black and white, as opposed to the even gray-scale of the rural environment. The dense *mise-en-scène* of the factory setting differs from the rural landscapes' open spaces; even the smoke seems to help fill the frame with dark graphics in the factory. There is movement in virtually all the shots, whether as billowing smoke (sometimes portrayed in under-cranked shots) or workers energetically stoking the furnaces. This differs from the near stasis of the pastoral images in sequences 1 and 2. The energy of sequence 3 carries over into an accelerated editing pace. The montage of workers stoking the cauldron, for example, has an average shot length of slightly more than 2 seconds (twenty-three shots in 47 seconds). These elements all combine to produce a sense of energy associated with this industrial setting, unlike the pastoral repose of the village. It indicates that the Lad has entered a more dynamic world.

The increased dynamism of sequence 3 also highlights the revolutionary pre-conditions that will figure in the film's development. This energized factory environment, not the leisurely village existence, will breed political activism. The revolutionary movement would emerge from the industrial setting, Marxist doctrine predicted, not from the agrarian situation. The more dynamic life of industry would produce dialectical tensions, which in turn would foment unrest. That doctrinal position is given form in the film's opening sequences, and they, in turn, presage the movie's first scene of worker discontent. This involves the episode in which the Lebedev factory stockholder orders a worker punished over a petty incident. Other men at the site register the injustice and the offended worker considers striking back. But the Communist Worker intervenes to advise restraint. This is the Communist's first appearance in the film, and he is immediately identified with the mentoring function that derives from his advanced political knowledge. His reluctance to act in this situation would have been consistent with a Marxist–Leninist sense of proper political development. The workers' movement would not benefit from a spontaneous reaction to a single incident of injustice. Only when the workers are better organized to oppose capitalism systematically can they effect fundamental change. Part of the Communist's standing as mentor is to recognize both when to act and when to delay action.

This factory sequence includes another stylistic shift between the alternatives of open montage and continuity. It begins with the general montage of industrial life described above. Once the incident of the worker's punishment starts to take shape, Pudovkin shifts to continuity editing in the confined space of the foundry. Pudovkin organizes the confrontation according to protocols of 180-degree editing, with consistent screen direction in glances, gestures and movements. The strategy ties the participants together in the mini-drama; the confrontation between the stockholder and the worker plays out as a shot/reverse-shot exchange, and the glance-reaction shots of the other workers confirm their response to the injustice. This tighter editing gives the incident its sense of drama, but it also fits Pudovkin's pattern of moving from the general to the specific. The opening montage of the sequence is designed to offer an overall impression of factory life, to typify the modern industrial situation. A title even generalizes from this setting by invoking workers of the 'Putilov, Obukhov, and Lebedev' factories (an echo of the 'Penza, Novgorod, Tver' title in sequence 1). The subsequent anecdote with the stockholder and worker is to provide a case study excerpted from that environment, a specific example of injustice produced by that larger industrial situation.

Sequence 4: Stock Market

When Pudovkin moves to the stock market and the Lebedev offices, he completes his survey of Russian economic relations. Prior scenes of rural and factory life cover the agricultural and industrial sectors of the economy. The stock market on display in sequence 4 represents the financial sector. The sequence also introduces representatives of the bourgeois and capitalist classes, whose presence complements the peasant and laboring classes depicted in sequences 1 and 3. But these are not co-equal economic spheres. Sequence 4 is designed to indicate that the financial community, including Lebedev, controls the rest of the economy under capitalism's uneven distribution of power.

The sequence is staged and edited so as to produce a sense of energy, which heightened activity translates into manipulations of the economy. It opens with several long shots of traders outside the stock exchange. The shots are crowded with groups of men in similar suits and bowler

Figure 3

hats (Figure 3). Even though they are packed together in such shots, they manage to bustle about; their movements appear quick and agitated as they engage in rapid stock trades. These densely packed framings and short, rapid movements continue in the medium shots of smaller groups of traders. This *mise-en-scène* has several functions. The dense pattern differentiates this setting from the open, pastoral landscape of the peasantry (sequence 1) and also from the functional, industrial environment of the workers (sequence 3). The similar suits also distinguish the bourgeoisie from the working classes who wear more functional clothing. The traders' suits, in fact, constitute a class uniform and support an impression of conformity. And the traders duly act in conformity, in something of a herd mentality. When the Lebedev stock price is posted, for example, the stock traders all take out notepads in perfect unison to record the price. Much as they scurry about, however, their energy is non-productive. They do not actually make a product through their exertions, as the factory workers do in the factory sequence. The traders seem to hustle and bustle but stay contained within the larger group, as though controlled by some outside power.

The source of that power is identified when Pudovkin shifts to Lebedev's office. Pudovkin cuts abruptly from a long, high-angle shot of scores of stock traders to a straight-on, medium shot of Lebedev's torso.

Lebedev is framed in such a way that his thick chest fills much of the frame (Figure 4). The transition involves a radical shift in angle and shot scale, from a dense matrix of small figures to a single, massive torso. And the energy of the crowd gives way to stasis, as Lebedev sits stock-still. These abrupt shifts in shot scale and graphics help define the power of Lebedev relative to that of the traders. His single form eclipses their many smaller forms in the power hierarchy, and he exerts authority without expending energy.

The application of that power is shown in subsequent shots. From the medium shot of Lebedev, Pudovkin cuts away to a long shot of the office interior. Lebedev remains in his static pose in a chair close to the left-center of the frame. He is balanced by the figure of an assistant on the frame's right-center. Both are surrounded by the considerable empty space of the large office. Again the relative stasis of the shot and its open space contrast with the denser graphics of the stock market images. Lebedev calmly dictates instructions to his assistant for stock transactions based on his new government contracts, and his pose never changes. But Pudovkin intercuts this location with more shots of the stock market crowds. The traders' movements are even more accelerated than before; they dash down corridors, for example. The intercutting makes them

Figure 4

seem to be responding to Lebedev's instructions, and their heightened activity appears to be a direct response to his calm dictation.

This staging defines Lebedev's power, and it differentiates his class from the laboring classes of workers and peasants. The latter groups engage in manual labor; they literally sell the energy and the manual skills of their bodies. Those skills are on display in sequences 1 and 3, and Pudovkin makes clear that the laboring classes must exert considerable personal energy to perform their tasks. Lebedev, by contrast, is a sedentary figure, barely moving his ample body, beyond making occasional phone calls. He buys and sells the labor of others, something he is shown doing through his trade and work orders. And while the individual worker can rely only on his own body to perform jobs, Lebedev is supported by a network of associates. He gives instructions to others – brokers, the factory manager, clerks – who exist in a hierarchical administrative apparatus. They carry out his will, relieving him of the obligation to expend any energy.

When Lebedev receives a phone message about his rising stock values, however, he finally moves. But even this movement is not one of productive labor, it is a sign of authority. In a quick, dramatic gesture, Lebedev leaps to his feet when he learns of his stock's value. Pudovkin emphasizes the movement with quick cuts of the chair overturning and items spilling on the floor. Pudovkin had repressed movement in this setting to save it for this moment. The powerful upward thrust of Lebedev's body becomes the physical manifestation of Lebedev's increased power, his rising stock value. In the earlier passage at the stock market, a trader remarked, 'Lebedev is going up!' This phrasing is something of metonymic play on words involving both the man and his company: as his company's stock goes up so does his personal power. The image of Lebedev leaping up seems designed to make this trope literal. Pudovkin then reinforces this impression of power by cutting from Lebedev on his feet to the Bronze Horseman statue of Peter the Great. The framing of Lebedev's head and shoulders matches that of the statue; both are shown from below as projections of authority. They even wear similar facial expressions. The statue was introduced earlier in the film to invoke the tsarist heritage; it is St Petersburg's most famous icon of imperial authority. It is linked with Lebedev to connect the traditional political power of the monarch to the new form of power provided by capital. The connection between political and industrial power will be further developed in the episodes on the war (sequence 15 – Attack) and the Provisional Government (sequence 18).

Figure 5

Sequences 6–8: Worker's Apartment; Strike; Meeting in the Worker's Apartment

In the first passage concerning the Wife and her family, Pudovkin turns to the modest lives of common workers, the population affected by the kind of economic manipulations on display in the previous episode at the stock market. In the course of three related sequences shifting between the Wife's apartment and the factory, Pudovkin replays the specific–general dynamic that characterized the episodes at the village (sequence 1) and the factory (sequence 3). As in those earlier episodes, Pudovkin shows both the living conditions of the family and the economic situation that produced those conditions. The passage begins at the Wife's flat and reveals the austere circumstances in which she and her children must live. Pudovkin then moves to an external explanation of those circumstances, the labor unrest at the factory. In making that move, he again shifts from continuity editing to montage.

The passage opens with the arrival of the Lad and an elderly peasant woman at the Wife's flat. They spend time moving through the workers' suburb before locating and entering the particular apartment that is their destination. These movements allow Pudovkin to depict the environment in which the Wife and her family must live; both the apartment and its surroundings are put on display. The arrival of the Lad and woman is shown in a set of exterior shots. Those views take in the large, austere buildings of the area. The shots' framings seem to dwarf the two small travelers relative to the massive buildings. These oblique-angle shots make the building loom up over the two human figures (Figure 5), continuing a pattern of city monuments towering over them during their journey across St Petersburg (cf. Figure 2). The implication of an alien, oppressive environment carries over from the city's landmarks to the workers' neighborhood. But these tenement buildings are severe in their design. The straight lines and right-angles of the buildings' crude, international-style architecture, contrasts with the ornamental ingredients of St Petersburg's landmark buildings. (Many of the city's public buildings were done in ornate baroque or neoclassical styles.) The massive forms of the tenement walls block off light – a sharp shadow line is articulated in the image of the courtyard – and produce an austere, gray effect throughout this environment, evoking the spartan existence of the families who must inhabit such an area.

That severe *mise-en-scène* carries over into the Wife's basement apartment. Its cold, gray walls are without decoration. The room's single street-level window offers little natural light. The only furnishings are a simple wood-block table, two wall benches and a bed. Otherwise the floor space of the setting is empty. The impression is one of empty floor space abruptly blocked off by dark walls. The door is insulated only with a layer of burlap, a makeshift arrangement against the cold. Otherwise, the space is without any softer textures; everything in the environment seems to have a dark and dank surface (Figure 6).

Certainly, a sense of coldness is the net effect of this *mise-en-scène*, and that carries over into the visage of the figure who is primarily connected to this environment, the Wife. The scene in the apartment introduces her character and implies that she has been hardened by living under such material circumstances. She coolly greets the Lad and old woman and refuses to share food with them. She reserves her precious potatoes for her own family rather than outsiders, but she even strikes her own daughter in the course of the meal. Her behavior throughout the scene suggests repressed anger at her circumstances tempered by her immediate responsibility to her family. The scene sets up a causal connection between material conditions and personal psychology, with the character's outlook on life reflecting her setting.

The scene inside the apartment uses continuity devices to develop this understanding of the Wife's character. Again, Pudovkin omits an establishing shot and situates a point-of-view character in the space, using glances and reaction shots to convey that character's immediate experi-

Figure 6

ence. Primary attention falls on the Wife's attitude, but the Lad's passive response is also evidenced in the exchanges. Once the Lad and old woman enter the apartment, they are relegated to a side bench and not allowed at the table where food will be served. The Wife feeds her daughter at that location. The modest meal is made to assume enormous prominence in the confines of this small living space. In a series of matched glances between the two figures on the bench and the Wife and child at the table, the potatoes emerge as the literal center of attention. The Lad and old woman stare passively at the table and their glances match up with the potatoes served from a bowl in the table's center. Meanwhile, the Wife looks back warily at the two uninvited guests. Two issues are registered in these applications of the Kuleshov effect. The travelers are hungry but abject; they stare at the food but make no gesture to proclaim their hunger. Meanwhile, the Wife's response suggests someone who has been hardened by want. Her reaction shots convey wariness about outsiders who might diminish her family's modest resources.

Even the choice of potatoes as the primary meal item is significant. It is the most humble of meals. It is even more basic than the bread consumed in the village scene, which is at least a processed food item. But for all their simplicity, the potatoes are made to seem enormous to characters whose living standard has been so constrained. Furthermore, this food,

Figure 7

which would have been grown and harvested by peasants, should connect the Wife with the two peasant visitors. But in an ironic turn, Pudovkin makes the food seem divisive. The suggestion, of course, is that the tsarist economy and its privations divide worker and peasant. Part of the political education that the Lad and the Wife will experience through the course of the film will be to appreciate the connection between the peasantry and proletariat. And that connection will be confirmed by a reappearance of the potato motif in the film's final moments.

At the end of the food incident in the apartment, the Wife reveals her motive for not sharing. She explains that her family's shortage will be made worse because, 'At the factory people are making trouble.' This line heralds a shift to the Lebedev factory and an abrupt change in editing style. In an elliptical montage passage, Pudovkin shows several factory images: billowing smoke, turning wheels, driving piston rods. The movement within the shots and the quick editing contrast with the relative stasis of the scene inside the apartment. And this image array has no point-of-view character or narrative focal point. This is factory life generally, not a cohesive space like the Wife's flat. What goes on here is different in character from what transpires in the Wife's environment, but the two locales are causally connected, as Pudovkin implies by the two scenes' juxtaposition. What happens in the factory world affects the Wife and her children. Their life inside the home answers to forces outside the home, namely the industrial economy. This causal connection is clarified as the scene plays out. The factory montage gives way to the staging of a strike, the factory 'trouble' alluded to by the Wife. The opening sequence showed the effect of the agricultural economy on a single family in a village; sequences 6 and 7 make a parallel connection between industry and a single household, this time in the urban environment.

The strike scene's editing involves a variant of the classical style. A montage of factory images and protesting workers gives way to a confrontation between workers and the plant manager in a factory yard. The manager announces a work speed-up to help fill Lebedev's new government contracts, and the workers resist the order. Out of this group emerges the Communist Worker to call for a strike. The confrontation is staged as though in a shot/reverse-shot pattern. The manager looks offscreen left and downward and the workers look back up and slightly to screen-right. But Pudovkin makes the scale of the exchange intentionally inconsistent (whereas conventional reverse-angle editing usually preserves consistent shot scale). Workers are shown in extreme long shot, with many small faces crowded into the frame (Figure 7). The factory boss, by contrast, is framed at an acute angle in medium shots, and his torso fills the frame along a diagonal from the upper-left to the lower-

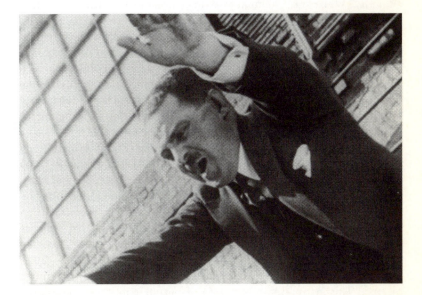

Figure 8

right of the frame (Figure 8). The impression is that he somehow looms up over the huddled mass of workers, as though suspended in air. This spatial relationship might be hard to reproduce in three-dimensional reality, but its dramatic function is to stress the boss's power relative to that of the workers. His gaze down commands more space and power than the reverse-angle gazes of the workers looking back up. The configuration evokes their respective stations in life.

Pudovkin adjusts this imbalance, however, when the Communist Worker emerges to lead the strike. The Communist seems literally to rise out of the assembled workers when he apparently steps on a platform to lift his torso above the heads of his peers in the factory yard. This elevates him above lens height so that his body fills much of the frame's left side. Then in a slightly low-angle shot, he extends his arm and speaks back in the direction of the plant manager. This pose, with its lower-left-to-upper-right diagonal line, mirrors that of the manager (Figure 9). The Communist Worker assumes roughly the same graphic authority as that of the factory boss. By making this adjustment in shot scale and graphics, Pudovkin offers the first suggestion of proletarian empowerment, with the Communist Worker emerging from the workers to improve their (literal and figurative) standing.

The subsequent montage seems to confirm this new measure of authority. When the Communist Worker declares the strike, Pudovkin intercuts shots of the Communist's defiant pose, arm extended, with images of the machines stopping. The flywheels and piston arms that had operated with such energy earlier in the scene grind to a halt. We see no one actually turn a switch or adjust a lever to stop the machinery. The editing suggests that the objects stop in immediate response to the Communist's strike proclamation, as though that alone brings the factory to a halt. Authority seems to emanate directly from the Communist Worker and to affect the industrial environment around him.

The last scene of the strike is an extreme long shot of a large group of motionless workers. Pudovkin then fades to black and fades back up on a shot inside the apartment showing the Wife's daughter and baby. This transition connects the factory realm and the domestic realm, reminding us that the strike will impinge on this family, specifically on these children, by further reducing their living standard. That sense of an outside force affecting this household is re-emphasized when the Communist Worker and a group of strikers enter the flat. They gather around the family table to convene an impromptu strike committee meeting. This act marks an incursion of outside political reality on the sanctuary of the home. The Wife's effort to preserve the apartment as a

Figure 9

protected, private space has given way to this meeting, which is political in nature. And significantly, the political meeting takes place at the table, the space previously reserved for domestic activity (feeding a child).

This motivates a new deployment of space in the scene. The Communist and his strike committee occupy the flat's central space at the table. The Lad remains on a bench to the left, in the same spot he occupied in sequence 6. (The older peasant woman is now gone, her disappearance never explained.) The Wife moves over to a space to the right of the table, in response to her baby's cry. That area contains a bed where the baby had been sleeping. The Wife picks up the baby and comforts it while sitting on the bed. The apartment is now divided into three separate zones: the Lad on the left, the men in the middle, and the Wife and baby on the right. The three zones are connected by continuity devices. The scene contains no master shot to reveal the location of the separate zones; they never all appear in a single take. Instead, glances back and forth among the participants suggest their relative locations, and the glances consistently obey the 180-degree rule. Pudovkin's staging isolates the three main figures in separate areas, but his continuity techniques confirm their proximity. The matched glances also confirm that the characters observe each other's activities, and their responses to those actions are indicated in reaction shots. More specifically, the staging

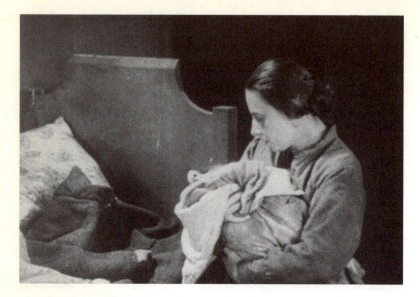

Figure 10

makes the Communist Worker's meeting the center of attention and highlights the reactions of the Lad and Wife who watch it unfold.

This deployment serves to develop the film's theme of political education within the character triad. This is the first time all three main characters figure in the same sequence, and their respective roles in the issue of political enlightenment are established. The Communist, in his mentoring function, occupies the central space. Significantly, he engages in a political endeavor, labor activism. That model of activism is available to be observed by the other two central characters, positioned on either side. Reaction shots reveal their response to that model, and at this early point in the film they have yet to comprehend its benefits. The Lad only stares back impassively, apparently not comprehending the significance of the actions taking place before him. His body language reinforces this impression; he sits slumped and motionless. The Wife, who had to surrender the family dining table, retreats to another space that evokes domesticity, the bed. This reconfirms her standing as someone responsible for domestic rather than public-sphere activities. Her response to the proletarian activism is one of resistance. She reasserts that her first priority is to her immediate family, not to the larger well-being of the proletariat. Her reaction shots even indicate anger directed at the strike committee (and at her own husband). She openly criticizes the strike for taking food from the mouths of her children, not recognizing that it will have larger, long-term benefits for working-class families. The scene's reverse-angle editing thus establishes the Lad's political *naïveté* and the Wife's narrow, family-centered sense of reality, two sets of views that will evolve through the course of the film into fuller political consciousness.

It is especially significant that the Wife attends to her baby during this scene. In holding the infant, she reasserts her primary identity as mother. The image of her cradling the baby evokes the Madonna-like poses of religious imagery (Figure 10). That pose would have doubtless been familiar to Russian audiences through exposure to religious iconography. Here the pose is secularized, turned into a suggestion of basic maternal protection, made the more pressing by the harsh circumstances this mother and child must endure.[4] As we will see, the Wife will repeat that cradling gesture at the film's conclusion (sequence 23). There it will mark a reconciliation. Here it evokes only her immediate commitment to family. Part of the Wife's political education will involve her eventual willingness to look beyond the boundaries of home and family, to recognize her larger class identity.

Sequence 9: Strikebreakers

The Wife and Lad's educations commence through a series of problems they experience in sequences 9–12. Their political *naïveté*, especially that of the Lad, is put on display in these episodes, resulting in further exploitation and attendant crises that begin to make them aware of the consequence of that exploitation. This process begins when the Lad ends up joining the strikebreakers in sequence 9, thus unwittingly pitting himself against the Communist Worker and the interests of the proletariat. Pudovkin makes it clear that the Lad's motives are never venal; he stumbles into the situation precisely because he lacks the political sophistication to appreciate the consequences of his actions.

In the episode on the strikebreakers, the Lad simply tries to follow the advice that he must seek employment. After all, he had been dispatched from his home village to work in industry, and the Wife had admonished him in the apartment sequence to 'get out and find work'. With no prospects other than poverty, the Lad enters the ranks of replacement workers at the Lebedev factory. Up to this point in the film, the Lad's character has been constructed as reactive rather than proactive. He takes no initiative but only follows the directions of others, usually in desultory fashion. Actor Ivan Chuvelev's interpretation of the character – with his placid expression, slumped posture and slow, uncertain walk – signifies passivity. His movements create a sense of weight bearing down on him, and they connote the absence of energy or initiative. He is a character who submits to the will of others, and that makes him subject to political exploitation. It explains how he ends up in such circumstances as prison and war in subsequent scenes (sequences 13 and 15). His function in the film, at least throughout the first half, is to represent something of a lumpen sensibility, as opposed to the more sophisticated proletarianism evidenced by the Communist Worker. The Lad's activities, such as they are, suggest the political problems posed by uninformed, lumpen proletarians, who inadvertently undermine the possibility of progressive change.

The Lad's confused efforts continue when he inadvertently betrays the strikers. A scuffle involving strikers, replacement workers and management personnel in the factory yard results in police intervention. The Lad speaks up to place blame for the labor trouble on one of the union organizers, the 'Bald One', as he is identified. The Lad specifically omits mention of the Communist Worker and seems concerned to shift blame to another strike supporter, so as to spare his acquaintance any trouble. He is hauled before the factory manager and coerced into revealing where the labor agitators can be found. Police then invade the Communist Worker's flat to arrest all the strike leaders, including the Communist Worker.

This sequence of events derives from the Lad's first efforts at initiative. He seems concerned to do the proper thing as others would have defined it. Under a system of conventional morality, he has taken 'correct' action in this sequence, first by seeking work (self-improvement) and then by co-operating with the authorities (respect for law). But the point of these narrative incidents is precisely to convey the argument that such conventional morality provides an instrument of exploitation. It results in the repression of the strike and the arrest of labor leaders. The Lad's actions are uninformed by political considerations, hence the unintended consequences. Pudovkin inserts the lesson at this point to provide a negative example of individual action against which one can measure the more beneficial instances that will be on display later in the film.

Part of the Lad and Wife's political education involves dealing with such flawed personal actions. Sequences 9–11 convey this through exchanges between the two characters. The arrest episode ends with a confrontation between the Wife and the Lad outside her apartment. The Lad stands alone in the courtyard, isolated from the tenement inhabitants. The Wife reproaches the Lad after learning of her husband's arrest. She walks toward the Lad in the courtyard, confronts him face-to-face in a quick set of reverse-angle close-ups, and then in a two-shot she violently shakes him. Tenement dwellers gaze out of their windows down at the

Lad in the courtyard as he endures this rebuke. He sheepishly looks back up at their accusing stares. The reverse-angle exchanges make him the object of their glances. Their scorn is conveyed through reaction shots, as is his humiliation. The staging is designed to make him a public example of failure, and the glances assign to him the conditions of humiliation and shame. He even carries a coin as a Judas-like sign of guilt after the plant manager gave him money in return for betraying the strikers. His humiliation will offer the first of many lessons he will have to learn on the path to consciousness.

Sequences 10–11: Confrontation with Merchant; Lad and Wife

Sequences 10 and 11 continue the exchanges between the Lad and Wife and extend the characters' political lessons. In sequence 10, the Wife tries unsuccessfully to secure provisions at a shop. Since her husband is in jail and unable to provide for the family, she must seek credit, but she is rebuffed by the shopkeeper. She angrily denounces him and exits the shop, proclaiming that the shopkeeper is 'part of the rottenness, too'. Then she warns him, 'But wait, wait.'

The merchant is included in the film as capitalism's merchant-class counterpart to the Lebedev character. He is part of Pudovkin's strategy of offering parallels between the situation of the Communist Worker in the realm of labor and the Wife's situation in the domestic realm. Just as her husband must deal with Lebedev's organization in his capacity as laborer, the Wife must deal with the merchant in her capacity as a family provider. The Wife even holds her baby in a way that harkens back to the maternal image in sequence 8 and reminds us of her familial responsibility. The merchant provides the most visible sign of capitalism's presence for the Wife, and his actions affect her just as Lebedev's affect the factory workers. The Wife's comment that the merchant is 'part of the same rottenness' indicates a new recognition on her part of how the capitalist system works. She begins to see parallels between the merchant and Lebedev, connections between different sectors of the capitalist order. And her parting warning to 'wait, wait' hints at her eventual commitment to political action. It specifically predicts the fact that she will participate in the bread riots of February 1917 in sequence 17 and will thus extract some revenge against the merchant class. More generally, it hints at her realization of the need for proletarian action and thus marks a stage in her political education.

The Lad's progress toward enlightenment is more protracted. His path includes additional well-meaning but misguided actions of the sort shown in sequence 9. He goes to the Wife's flat in sequence 11 out of concern over the Communist Worker's arrest. There he offers the Wife the same coin he had received as payment for implicating the strike leaders, apparently believing that the money would make amends for her husband's arrest. The Wife angrily rejects the money, recognizing its tainted nature. In the course of offering the coin, the Lad approaches the Wife who sits at the same table where she had previously fed her daughter. The Lad places the coin on the table to make his offer. That gesture harkens back specifically to the scene with the potatoes: both incidents make the table the center of attention, and both scenes use material items – the potatoes in one and the coin in another – to signify the detrimental effect of capitalism on this family. It is worth noting that there is no food on the table in this second incident (recall the Wife's failure to procure food in sequence 10). The money effectively replaces the potatoes in that space – currency in lieu of consumable goods. Ironically, had the Wife possessed this currency in the prior scene, she would have been able to purchase food. But she specifically rejects this monetary offer, since the money is connected to the Lebedev system. Her gesture marks her growing awareness of the system's corruption, including the extent to which it exploits workers through such meager rewards.

Sequence 12: Fight at Lebedev's Office

The Lad's equivalent recognition will come only after additional crises. He goes to the Lebedev headquarters in sequence 12 to request that the Communist Worker be released from prison. This gesture is still motivated by a sense of personal responsibility rather than a larger appreciation of proletarian solidarity. It is prompted by the Lad's guilt-laden confrontations with the Wife (sequences 9 and 11). Pudovkin thus offers the Lad's run-in with Lebedev as another instance of misdirected individual action. Once again the Lad takes some private initiative only to see it fail when he lands in jail. But it provides another necessary stage in the Lad's evolution. This negative case of flawed personal action can be measured against the more successful examples of informed action evident later in the film.

The scene in the Lebedev office warrants some elaboration. It involves another shift from continuity into a discontinuous editing style, moving toward more fragmented editing as the fight takes shape. The scene's rising energy level finds its complement in rapid, disjunctive cutting.

When the Lad first enters the office, Pudovkin shows Lebedev and several office workers reacting to his presence. The Lebedev employees each individually turn and look offscreen in the general direction of the Lad's arrival. Each glance takes a slightly different angle in rough approximation to where the person is positioned in the office. The effect is that of a circle of figures looking at the Lad, who would be more or less in the middle. That effect is sustained by a subsequent long shot which shows the Lad surrounded by a circle of several office workers as he pushes his way into the area. The clerks then give way as the Lad confronts Lebedev and the factory manager. At this point the Lad is made a point-of-view character; in a series of glances he looks at Lebedev, the manager, and then back toward the various office workers who have slipped into the background. Without using an establishing shot to convey the characters' locations, Pudovkin's reverse-angle edits have sustained an impression of the Lad encircled by the various members of the Lebedev staff.

When the fighting breaks out, however, the space around the Lad begins to warp. The Lad tussles with the plant manager and throws him aside, and that action seems to create an energy that radiates out to the rest of the office. In a series of shots with often inconsistent screen direction, we see workers running about, items of furniture overturning, people shouting. One pattern that Pudovkin maintains through the central part of the fight involves medium shots of the Lad's face and upper torso juxtaposed with some violent action elsewhere in the vicinity. For example: (1) Lad throws manager aside (movement); (2) Manager falls by desk (movement); (3) Medium shot of Lad (stationary); (4) Clerks running down corridor (movement); (5) Clerk waving arms (movement); (6) Medium shot of Lad (stationary); (7) Manager getting up (movement); (8) Medium shot of Lad shouting (stationary). This montage pattern thus balances stationary images of the Lad (shots 3, 6, 8) with energized shots of figures around him (shots 1, 2, 4, 5, 7). Once again, he seems to occupy some fixed position in the imaginary space of this event while objects and people spiral off from his body. His solid, central figure contrasts with the chaotic, disjunctive movements around him.

The scene opens in continuity with the suggestion of the Lad physically encircled by members of the Lebedev staff. Then that tidy circle is disrupted by the Lad's presence. He is there to confront Lebedev directly, but he must also deal with the array of Lebedev minions. And they seem to engage him from all directions. Much of the Lebedev hierarchy – alluded to in sequence 4 – is involved in the confrontation, including the plant manager, some middle-level employees and even a typist. Eventually the police intervene, connecting Lebedev's power to that traditional institution of order. In fact, when the police haul the Lad away to his arrest, they encircle him, thus repeating the circle motif and connecting the police with the Lebedev workers who had previously surrounded the

Lad. This is the only time in the film that Lebedev, the personification of capitalism, must deal directly with a representative of the toiling classes, in this case the Lad. But his administrative hierarchy intervenes, in a staging that reminds one of capitalism's support system. A single worker like the Lad is overmatched while acting in isolation.

More important, however, might be the suggestion that the Lad's raw anger is undirected and thus useless as a political instrument against capitalism. This brand of personal, spontaneous lashing-out against injustice produces only chaos, as evidenced by the scene's progressively fragmented style. The Lad lacks an informed course of action that would produce real political change. Recall that the Communist Worker had advised an angry colleague early in the film not to react spontaneously against injustice but to wait for other workers to organize (sequence 3). The Lad's action in sequence 12 seems designed to confirm the wisdom of that advice.

Indeed, the Lad's actions through much of the film's first section yield detrimental outcomes, whether imposing on the Wife (sequence 6), seeking work (sequence 9), or confronting Lebedev (sequence 12). Such incidents put his uninformed, lumpen sensibility on display. That sensibility will be refined in the film's subsequent sections into lessons in how the individual can be empowered through political awareness and how his actions can produce more beneficial results.

II. War Period

The beginning of section II on the war period marks a change in the story tempo of *The End of St Petersburg*. Whereas section I provided representative situations of Russian life in a time generally identifiable as the late-imperial era, with the stories of three representative citizens highlighted within that context, the latter two sections have more precise historical markers to help spectators register the advance of story time: the dating of the First World War, the February Revolution, the advent of the Provisional Government and the October Revolution. Narrative incidents in the latter two sections move at a swifter pace, as though a sweep of historical events, including the energy of the revolutionary movement, takes over with a new momentum. And the fictional lives of the three main characters go through more pronounced changes in response to this accelerated narrative progress. The developmental patterns of political education and enhancement take pronounced shape as the characters respond to the dynamic revolutionary forces on display in the film's latter sequences.

Sequence 14: 'Mother Russia Calls!'

Sequence 14 opens with a three-and-one-half minute montage on Russia's entry into the First World War and the nation's initial war fever, and it thus provides one of those historical markers of events that will change the characters' lives. It begins rather cryptically. It does not start out with, say, an intertitle dating the moment as August 1914 (the outbreak of hostilities) or show some obvious, official act such as Tsar Nicholas II issuing Russia's war declaration. Rather it begins with a montage of nocturnal images of St Petersburg, shots of cannon juxtaposed with the city skyline, images of phone lines, and then a late-night phone message received by an army officer in his bed. The caller's identity and the phone call's exact contents are not revealed. But the call is followed by the caption 'Mother Russia calls!', a patriotic slogan from the war years. The juxtaposition thus equates that slogan with the phone message, as though 'Mother Russia' literally calls by phone. The audience is left to infer that the image array signifies war. That inference is reinforced when the officer receiving the message promptly climbs out of bed. Then the cannon shown in stasis in a previous shot is elevated as though raising its sights. Thus, the line 'Mother Russia calls!' seems to animate both the men and the instruments of war.

This opening sets up two patterns. Things begin slowly in the sequence, with long takes and quiet, nocturnal images, and then give way to frenzied activity and hectic editing later in the sequence, as a society at peace is transformed by the hysteria that yields war. Also the sequence has no single agent of action or point-of-view character; it is comprised of images of several miscellaneous locations around St Petersburg. It does have a certain linear quality in that the phone lines, phone call and reaction to the call articulate causal linkages. But it is not as though this is a particular phone message from a particular person. The origin of the message is never shown, and, as noted, we do not see Tsar Nicholas or his ministers as the source of a war proclamation. This disjunctive opening provides a generalized, abstract representation of war's onset, as though it is a historical event that is beyond the control of any identifiable human. Indeed, Soviet doctrine held that the war was not the product of a single human agent – Archduke Ferdinand's assassin notwithstanding – but the logical outgrowth of capitalism. Imperialism was the last stage of capitalism's historical development, Lenin had held, and the 1914 hostilities ushered in the great 'Imperialist War', the sign that the imperial powers of Europe were turning on each other and thus helping bring about capitalism's eventual collapse.[5] Pudovkin seems determined to locate the war's origin in such broad,

Figure 11

anonymous forces, a strategy which takes material shape in this sequence as generalizing images of militarism.

That impression is sustained through the rest of sequence 14. After the phone message, the sequence gives way to representations of the military, but Pudovkin is careful not to link these to any particular character or locale. In fact, he seems determined to decontextualize the images, to make them representations of a general concept, in this case militaristic patriotism. That concept takes shape in a series of five shots of torsos of uniformed men. The figures are all framed so that their heads are cut off. Their chests are bedecked with massive arrays of medals and braid, so much so as to parody military regalia (Figure 11). Their broad chests and dense medal arrays convey a sense of weight. The figures either sit still or move with exaggerated slowness in their chairs, adding to the impression of heaviness. If anything, these bulky, stationary figures remind one of statues rather than real, animate people. In fact, a statue of the bulky Tsar Alexander III is shown later in the sequence. He was a nineteenth-century monarch remembered for his reactionary views and harsh, imperialist policies. The statue's broad chest and the framing of the torso remind one of the generals' heavy bodies in this episode, thus connecting the generals with the film's motif of statuary. As noted, Pudovkin uses statuary in the film to convey Russia's imperial legacy, and that certainly carries over to the Alexandrine allusion. The statue and its framing also recall the thick torso of Lebedev in sequence 4, whose industry sustains the war (cf. Figure 4). Through these various cross-references, Pudovkin thus connects the war's outbreak with capitalism and (its final stage) imperialism.

From these heavy, sedentary forms, sequence 14 moves to more energetic figures as the war momentum builds. Close and medium shots show men in exterior settings blowing trumpets, beating drums, clashing cymbals and playing wind instruments. These shots of highly animated musicians are intermixed with long shots of crowds waving and cheering. The waving arms match the motion of banners blowing in the wind. This passage has movement (waving arms, swaying banners, musical strokes) and noise (both crowd noise and music are invoked by the imagery) as its dominant impressions. (The original music track for this scene also added to the impression of cacophony with a distorted, off-key rendering of the Russian national anthem.)[6] It shows the propagation of the war fever among the population, and that fever is represented as an energy that passes from the band to the crowd and which is signified by accelerated motions. The waving spectators actually seem to pick up the rhythms of the musicians in their movements.

For the duration of this sequence Pudovkin separates his image array from the experience of any individual agent. The sequence is an exercise in intellectual cinema, as it advances a general, rhetorical point about war rather than following the activities of a fictional character.[7] It treats patriotism and militarism as sentiments that are manufactured and propagated by officialdom. This is suggested through the sequence's overall design, which starts within official situations (the phone message, the generals and officials), is taken out to the streets (band, speakers), and then is picked up by the general population (crowd reactions). Pudovkin paces the sequence to suggest a rising level of hysteria. He starts out slowly with quiet nocturnal images and shots of nearly immobile generals, and he then moves to the highly energized street scenes. The editing pace and the suggestions of noise increase in conjunction with that surge of activity. This demonstrates a process that develops a momentum beyond the control of any single agent, an impersonal social force in action.

In the middle of sequence 14, Pudovkin shifts from this abstract level back to the small-scale, by looking in, as it were, on the situation of the Lad. Pudovkin switches to the prison where the Lad has been incarcerated after the Lebedev tussle. The Lad and some other prisoners are pulled out of jail and promptly conscripted into the army as 'volunteers'. They then join a parade where the patriotic motifs are replayed ('Mother Russia calls!'). The Lad has been imprisoned for fighting and, in another ironic turn on his misguided actions, he is let out of prison to fight. As he is pulled out of his cell, the Lad has the familiar blank expression and heavy walk that characterized his behavior in the film's early sequences. This body language has been established as a sign of his passive response to forces he cannot control. In this scene it indicates that his conscription is a political act inflicted on him by an outside force. He and the other conscripts are being exploited by the war machine on display elsewhere in the sequence.

Recall how Pudovkin balanced the specific and the general in the scenes of the first encounter with the Wife (sequences 6–8). There he showed the Wife's situation, then examined labor conditions and then returned to her environment. Pudovkin does something similar here with episodes on the Lad, the war, and the Lad, noting the relationship between the large-scale historical phenomenon of war and the effect it has on the fate of one man. And in both cases, Pudovkin deploys intellectual montage to explore the large causal phenomena of labor unrest and war. The Lad is not an instigator of the war hysteria, just as the Wife does not control her family's economic situation. Both must cope with political forces that exceed their power, and such forces are explored through the montage aesthetic.

The latter part of sequence 14 involves a military parade that draws together several motifs from the previous montage passage on war fever. Prisoners and other conscripts are herded together into a ragged rank-and-file formation. One of the ex-prisoners carries a portrait of Nicholas II at the head of the formation and the title 'Mother Russia calls!' reappears. That slogan now comments ironically on the men's draft status; the conscripts have been 'called', as it were, into military service.

The parade involves a military unit, shown from above, marching through city streets. Cheering civilians gaze down from surrounding buildings at the street-level parade. The soldiers appear in uniform and in orderly ranks; the ragtag recruits have given way to this smart military formation, but the prior scene of the motley group of inductees does suggest that the soldiers come from lower-class origins. The cheering crowd is made up of the bourgeoisie. Class identity separates the soldiers and the on-lookers.

This separation is reinforced by a spatial disjunction in the editing. The spectators lean out of windows and over balconies to cheer from above. The soldiers walk along a city street somewhere below their gaze. Pudovkin uses reverse angles, showing the audience from below and the soldiers from above. But the angles do not match correctly. The spectators are too high, a sign of their exalted social status relative to the soldiers who will actually have to fight the war. The two spaces seem disconnected, despite the reverse angles. In fact, when spectators toss flowers down to the troops, the reverse-angle shots of the soldiers do not show the flowers alighting. Pudovkin here plays off conventions of continuity. He uses false reverse angles and false matches on action to articulate not spatial continuity, but a gap between the spectators and soldiers. Their relative political power supersedes their apparent physical proximity.

The spectators gazing down from the buildings also reside in an Art Nouveau environment that seems artificial and out of keeping with the environment of the soldiers. The *mise-en-scène* of the crowd contains garlands, flowers and banners, decorative touches that have soft textures and that sway gracefully in the breeze. These delicate, foliate forms contrast with the simple gray lines of the military unit. The spectators' over-emotional gestures and expressions – one elderly man ostentatiously wipes away tears – also connote artifice. Even the Alexandrine statue is covered in garlands, and a close shot of the statue's face reveals tears streaming down, as though the dead tsar is also overcome with the emotions of the moment. This comic turn parodies the ostentatious emotions of the bourgeois spectators. These disjunctions of editing and *mise-en-scène* make a rhetorical point about the power differential between classes. A bourgeois population supports war, but they will spectate rather than participate, hence their elevated position in an artificial environment. Workers and peasants will be sent to the trenches while these bourgeoisie will remain in a comfortable environment.

Sequences 15–16: Attack; War Drags On

Material on the First World War constitutes much of the balance of section II (sequences 15–16). The roles of the central characters diminish as Pudovkin broadens his narrative horizons during the war sequences. We briefly see the Communist and the Lad in the trenches as reminders of the fate of working men during the First World War: they would have had to serve in combat. But the war sequences provide a far-reaching explanation of the conflict's causes and consequences, which will then help motivate the revolutionary actions shown in the film's final section.

Sequence 15 represents the war experience through a complex, extended exercise in intellectual montage. It leaps between locales to associate the St Petersburg stock market with the battle front, and it thus links the activities of Lebedev and capitalism to the war's prosecution. The sequence begins with an elegant image of a rural landscape. It shows a horizon line running along the bottom edge of the frame with only a small hut in the left corner and flowing clouds to break up the graceful picture. Then that peaceful locale erupts violently when an artillery explosion consumes the entire setting, a quiet, pastoral image shattered by war. There follows a series of explosions and flames which signify mass destruction. The landscape virtually disappears from view in these subsequent shots; the film frame in each shot is substantially consumed by smoke, flame and debris. No specific time or place is assigned to this locale; an intertitle appearing 12 seconds into the sequence says simply 'the front', which title is followed by more shots of explosions. The opening few seconds seem designed to offer a general, almost archetypal image of destruction rather than a specific narrative incident (no human figure appears), and the laconic intertitle supports that generalizing tendency. This opening passage sets up a rhetorical stance on the war's indiscriminate destructiveness that will carry through the balance of the sequence.

That rhetorical mode takes more direct form via a set of three titles that follow this opening: 'In the name of the tsar!'; 'Of the Fatherland!'; 'AND OF CAPITAL!' These titles are juxtaposed with more images of explosions and billowing smoke. The title about capital is also preceded by a disturbing shot showing dead soldiers sliding down an embankment: the first sign of human presence in this environment is associated with death. The titles provide ironic commentary on the destruction by inserting patriotic slogans in the context of this death. The sequence puts particular emphasis on 'capital' as the source of the destruction; the last title invokes capitalism in the context of the dead bodies, and the text appears on the screen in capital letters for particular emphasis. Per the sequence's rhetorical tone, it puts forth a thesis, of sorts, in proposing that capitalism is responsible for the war's devastation. Pudovkin then uses intellectual montage to sustain that proposition.

The ensuing montage passage depicts a battle between German and Russian troops, as the two sides prepare for conflict and then commit to a fierce fight. Pudovkin intercuts this situation with footage set at the St Petersburg stock market and the Lebedev headquarters. This second line of footage does not have a linear development and need not necessarily be happening simultaneously with the battle. The connection between the two lines is causal rather than temporal. The suggestion is that the conduct of the capitalist war industry, including that of the Lebedev empire, puts these soldiers in harm's way and yields human suffering. That argument is fleshed out in several ways through intellectual montage.

One way involves parallels between German and Russian troops in the battle. This shifts blame for the war away from national identity and helps direct it back at capitalism through the implication that soldiers from both nations are victims. Preparations for the battle involve cross-national symmetries. For example, a title identifies a group of Russian soldiers as 'the people of Penza, Novgorod, and Tver', repeating the motif from earlier sequences on the backgrounds of peasants and workers. That motif then returns in a variant when some German troops appear and another title identifies them as 'people of Saxony, Württemburg, and Bavaria'. These parallel captions are matched by equivalencies in the accompanying shots. Soldiers from both sides are herded into their trench positions by their officers, and in each case the officer is framed alone from below while the soldiers are shown as anonymous lines of gray uniforms moving through the trenches. In a pause before the battle, Pudovkin shows particular soldiers in medium shots to give these figures some individual identity, and he intercuts images of both Russian and German troops tensely awaiting the order to attack. (The Communist Worker and the Lad appear among the Russian troops.) During the ensuing battle, Pudovkin intermixes shots of casualties from both armies.

While the parallels between German and Russian soldiers establish equivalency, the connection between the stock market and the battle is represented as causal. Pudovkin mixes those two lines so as to imply that actions at the stock exchange have consequences in the trenches. Puns on business activities carry over to the battle, for example. Preparations for the battle are followed by the title, 'The transaction begins', at which point Pudovkin shows not the stock exchange, but the first artillery exchange. At the battle's conclusion, a title declares, 'The transaction is complete', followed by a shot of a dead soldier. Another announces, 'Both parties [of the transaction] are satisfied', and we see shots of both Russian and German dead. During the height of the battle, a title asks rhetorically, 'What are we dying for?' A shot of a dying soldier precedes that text, as though he could have issued the question. Pudovkin then cuts back to the stock exchange. The next three shots are: steps of the exchange with numerous brokers moving about; stock quotes on a chalk board (Lebedev's stock goes up); Lebedev arriving at the market steps while the traders part respectfully to let him pass. These images provide the answer to the title's rhetorical question. The market, its pricing and Lebedev's dominance are all included in this three-shot answer. This combination of ingredients indicates the broader concept of capitalism as the answer to the question, but the passage also reminds one of Lebedev's specific role as the main war profiteer. The second of the three shots, the stock quotation, shows his company's value increasing. This is done in a dissolve in which one value is replaced by another, higher figure. But no human hand intervenes to erase the first price and record the second. The dissolve leaves undetermined how and why the price changes; the audience is left to make the connection, to infer that the war directly produces the increase and thus benefits Lebedev.

Various graphic matches also connect stock market activities to the fighting. Motion on the market steps, for example, imitates patterns in the battle footage. Shots of traders charging up the steps of the exchange building give way to images of soldiers scrambling out of their trenches and charging into battle; more punning intertitles – 'Over the top!' and 'Forward!' – comment on these parallel actions. Frantic trading at the exchange duplicates the fierce actions of combatants at the height of the battle. For example, a medium shot of a soldier slashing with his rifle and bayonet matches a medium shot of a broker shaking his arms wildly. The two lines of action even follow parallel emotional arcs; the trading activity builds in a crescendo of energy peaking at the same time that the battle reaches a climax. And Pudovkin cuts between the two threads of action more rapidly as the energy of each peaks.

If Pudovkin wants to leave the impression that capitalism's stock market controls the battleground, he leaves no doubt as to who controls the market. Lebedev's presence is privileged in this montage just as it was in first stock market sequence. As the battle is taking shape, Lebedev places phone orders to associates about financial transactions. In cutting between Lebedev and the mass of traders, Pudovkin replays the graphic mismatch used in the first stock market sequence. He once again shows Lebedev seated in a level shot, and then cuts abruptly to a high-angle shot of the mass of traders. From that high camera angle, the stock traders appear as a dense pattern of identical bowler hats rather than a group of individuals. The radical shift in shot scale is again designed to signify the power differential between Lebedev and the other brokers who simply follow his lead. This becomes salient in subsequent cuts that involve false sound cues. Pudovkin cuts from Lebedev on the phone to the mass of traders (or at least their hats), who seem to overhear the phone conversation. When Lebedev first speaks into the phone, the traders' miscellaneous movements promptly stop as though they are trying to listen. After a subsequent phone remark, their heads (hats) all turn at once as though hearing his remarks. Lebedev is at his office when he makes the call, not at the stock exchange; so the traders could not conceivably hear the instructions he issues over the phone. Rather the false reaction shots of the traders seeming to listen indicate the power Lebedev exercises over the market. The editing leaves the impression that the traders respond in absolute conformity to Lebedev's instructions.

That power connotation is reinforced when Lebedev finally arrives at the market. The moment is privileged. It is timed to take place immediately after the intertitle 'What are we dying for?', thus connecting Lebedev to the rhetorical question that sums up the sequence's argument about capitalism and war. When he arrives at the front steps of the exchange building, the thick mass of traders part as if in deference to his presence; in an almost comic image, the mass of dark suits and hats on the steps spread evenly and rapidly to make a path. When Lebedev enters the building, Pudovkin cuts back to the same high-angle shot of the mass of hats he had shown earlier in the sequence. As if on cue, the traders all lift their hats at once to salute Lebedev's presence. Pudovkin cuts from this gesture to shots of the dead and dying at the front. The salute signifies the traders' deference to Lebedev, but the juxtaposition also produces an impression that the traders celebrate the front-line deaths.

Significant by its absence from the battle scene is any reference to the military general staff. They were present only as headless torsos in the 'Mother Russia calls!' montage, and they do not appear in the battle scene at all. We see two lower-echelon officers herding men into trenches, but there is no representation of a command authority directing the battle once the fighting starts. Clearly Lebedev is meant to stand in for the general staff. Like a military commander, he gives out orders over a phone. In this case, his orders translate into the war industry actions that are then inflicted on soldiers through the combat experience they must endure. The power hierarchy worked out through this extended exercise in intellectual montage suggests that Lebedev controls the market which, in turn, controls military affairs. Recall also that Lebedev is sometimes depicted so as resemble both the bulky generals of sequence 14 and the Alexandrine statue. Lebedev is thus equated with both military and political authority. The implication is that military and political power reside in the realm of capital in the modern world.

As noted, the temporal relationship between the battle and the market activity is not articulated but is subordinated to the causal connection. Neither the date nor the location of the battle is clearly established. Rather than alluding to a specific assault, the battle is meant to be emblematic, to illustrate the kinds of hardships soldiers might have endured at any point in the war. The montage patterns in sequence 15 make a general case about the causes and consequences of the war, rather than offering a specific plot incident to advance the film's narrative.

In sequence 16, then, Pudovkin shows another common dimension of the war, the numbing experience of trench life. This impression of the soldiers' long, dreary routine in the trenches complements the ferocity of the battle experience in the prior passage. The trench sequence works through a montage pattern that uses temporal ellipses. It starts off with intertitles announcing that three years pass and more men are sent to the front. These are general claims that are then given quick verification through representative images of the war: a field covered with artillery smoke, a scarred battle landscape with dead bodies, soldiers in the trenches enduring a fierce rain. Such shots do not so much advance story time as indicate the typical moments the soldiers might have lived through across that three-year period.

In the second half of this short sequence, however, a narrative point takes shape that provides a transition to the film's final section on the revolutionary movement. This is a sign of growing discontent among the troops which will contribute to their eventual radicalization. A soldier is shown crouched in the trench during a downpour writing a letter. The letter's text appears in an intertitle: 'We've been fighting for three years and don't know what for.' This text picks up the what-are-we-fighting-for? motif of the battle scene in the previous sequence and recasts it as a problem of morale that erodes over time ('We've been fighting for three years ...'). This incident is followed by three discontinuous shots: a long shot of a cross marking a grave site; a medium shot of a tattered page of the communist organ *Pravda*, lying in a muddy trench; a medium shot of the grave shown earlier, close enough now to see a small sign that dates the grave as 1917. This seemingly laconic montage passage does several things. It confirms the finality of death for the soldiers, with the grave site rather than living beings offered as the last image of the war. The discarded *Pravda* implies that the men have been exposed to leftist propaganda, apparently through covert organizing efforts by communists in the ranks. It hints at the soldiers' possible radicalization through the war ordeal. Finally, the grave's date takes the story time to 1917, the moment when that radicalization takes shape as revolution. That provides the transition to the overt revolutionary action shown in the film's third section.

III. 1917 Revolutions

Much of section II on the war departs from the account of the central characters' development. We see the Lad and the Communist Worker only briefly in the trenches in sequence 15, and the Wife is omitted from the section entirely. Pudovkin casts his account of the war on a broad scope, as an epic event that affects the entire society. And appropriately the section includes his most ambitious application of the montage aesthetic. By placing the war as the middle section, Pudovkin gives it the pivotal narrative role of explaining how and why the masses would have developed revolutionary aspirations. They might have endured the privations of the tsarist order through section I, but the war-related crises of section II demonstrate the need for radical change. That lesson then motivates the broad-based revolutionary activity on display in section III. By briefly looking in on the Lad in the war scenes, Pudovkin at least reminds us that he was part of that ordeal and would have acquired that radical aspiration. Consistent with the theme of empowerment, he and the other central characters will play larger roles in the revolutionary events of section III.

Sequence 17 : February Revolution

Section III of *The End of St Petersburg* opens with a short montage of the Russian armaments industry at work. Specifically, Pudovkin shows artillery shells being polished as the last stage of their production. Two consecutive titles announce: 'Cannon shells, Cannon shells'; 'Instead of Bread'. That second title provides a transition to a depiction of the bread riots that swept St Petersburg in February 1917. The causal connection is made clear in this juxtaposition and in the rhetorical tone of the titles: as Russia's economy is drained of resources in the war effort, Russian civilians must suffer privation, and they are politically radicalized as a result.

Sequence 17 thus provides an account of the Russian home front that complements the impression of the soldiers' lot in sequence 16. We were left with evidence of the soldiers' growing discontent at the end of the war sequence. The bread riot episode reflects a similar process in the civilian sector, and this time women appear as the participants to balance the roles of the men in the war scenes. And just as Pudovkin had shown the armaments industry determining events at the front in sequence 15, here he shows it similarly controlling the civilian sector. Once again, Pudovkin assigns narrative causality to an overarching economic force, in this case capitalism's war industry.

Pudovkin also re-establishes in this sequence the pattern of returning periodically to the specific situation of a central character when he shows the Wife involved in the protests. She plays a prominent role in the event; as the women arrive at a shop with a sign announcing 'no bread or flour', the Wife calls out to other protesters and channels their anger into action. In response to her call, they storm the shop to expropriate food.

The Wife's actions in this sequence mark a major stage in her progress toward political consciousness and activism. Consistent with her prior identity as a provider, this phase of her development borrows from the food motif. But whereas the Wife had been denied bread by a merchant in the first scene at the shop (sequence 10), now she and others take more militant action to acquire provisions. The food motif traces her evolution from family provider in the scene with the potatoes (sequence 6), to frustrated consumer in the capitalist exchange system in the scene at the shop (sequence 10), to activist in the February Revolution (sequence 17).

The other sign of the Wife's development is her changed environment. She was initially identified with the apartment introduced in sequence 6. Her early character traits reflected the cold, severe characteristics of that setting. And the prison-cell quality of that apartment seemed almost to enclose her in a sealed chamber, walling her off from the outside world. She, in turn, treated the flat as a sanctuary, a place where she could protectively look after her children, and she clearly resisted others' incursions into that protected space. But in the later stages of the film she moves about more freely in open spaces: the streets during the February Revolution (sequence 17); the Winter Palace after the October Revolution (sequence 23). A sign of her empowerment is the greater freedom of action she enjoys as the film progresses. And her body language changes accordingly. She becomes more animated. The physical reserve that characterized her behavior in the first scene at the apartment gives way to more energy and to greater passion over political injustice. 'They [the merchants] are getting fat off us!', she angrily shouts and gestures to the other women protesters before leading their assault on the bread shop.

Sequence 18: Provisional Government

Pudovkin follows the February Revolution with a caricature of the Provisional Government. Soviet doctrine held that the February Revolution represented a bourgeois revolution. Although it was a necessary precursor of the final proletarian revolution of October, the February Revolution produced only a bourgeois regime in its immediate aftermath in the form of the Provisional Government. Pudovkin follows this line in his representation of Kerensky and his supporters in sequence 18. They appear as inhabitants of an artificial, bourgeois world, removed from the political reality of revolutionary Russia. In a configuration that evokes a theatrical setting, the scene shows Kerensky being applauded by representatives of the bourgeoisie dressed in evening clothes. The scene's staging clearly evokes the contrived quality of a theatrical performance; Kerensky seems to perform – a possible allusion to the real Kerensky's grandiose public

Figure 12

manner– while his wealthy admirers constitute an audience watching from the balcony of a theater.

The artifice of this bourgeois world is registered in various stylistic devices. For example, the scene's art design has a highly stylized Art Nouveau look (Figure 12). This sets the episode off from much of the rest of the film, which generally employs a stripped-down naturalism in its design schemes. The sets in sequence 17 are lit with *chiaroscuro* effects that also differ from the flat, even lighting used in most of the film's other scenes. Cinematographer Anatoli Golovnia's lighting actually produces a sheen on the bourgeois figures in Kerensky's audience. Their bodies receive highlights that make them seem almost to sparkle, to reflect light like the jewels worn by the women. To stress the decadence of this setting, Pudovkin inserts into the scene several images of death and destruction on the war front that were shown earlier in the film. These war inserts are in the raw documentary style of the battle scenes in sequences 15 and 16 and thus contrast sharply with this bourgeois setting. The inserts remind us of a hard reality that is missing from the fabricated environment of these social elites. Pudovkin even cuts in such a way as to connect these clapping, tuxedo-clad spectators with images of death at the front. Although they are cheering Kerensky, this juxtaposition makes them seem to applaud the loss of life.

While the style of this sequence differentiates it from much of the rest of the film, it does evoke comparison with one prior incident, the moment when the soldiers marched off to war to the cheers of spectators at the end of the 'Mother Russia calls!' montage (sequence 14). Both episodes use Art Nouveau design features, including flower motifs. Both have a bourgeois audience looking down on representatives of the military. (Kerensky wears his uniform, a sign of his status as the government's War Minister.) Some members of Kerensky's audience even reappear from the parade scene. Spectators express their adulation in exaggerated emotions in both situations. The Alexandrine statue seems to cry in the 'Mother Russia calls!' montage as does an elderly bourgeois man in the Kerensky scene. Such physical gestures as throwing flowers carry over from the one scene to the other as well, and certain shots from the 'Mother Russia calls!' montage (e.g. blaring trumpets) return as non-diegetic inserts in the Provisional Government episode. Even the intertitle 'Long Live the Provisional Government!' echoes the sloganeering of the phrase 'Mother Russia calls!'

The Kerensky sequence also uses disorienting spatial cues that might remind one of the parade. The spaces occupied by Kerensky and his audience do not match up properly. Kerensky stands alone on an open floor. He is shown from above in framings that stress the empty floor space around him. The audience members would appear to be above him in balconies of some sort. But no establishing shot puts the two areas into context. And when the spectators are shown in full shots, they are not positioned in a theatrical balcony but in spacious rooms. Pudovkin then uses continuity devices to seem to connect the locations, but the apparent eyeline matches and matches on action do not articulate a coherent space. Even the light falling on Kerensky is inconsistent with the stylized lighting of the bourgeois figures. As in the parade scene, Pudvokin uses continuity devices, but does so in order to create an artificial, rather than realistic sense of space.

These various gestures of connecting the Kerensky scene with the 'Mother Russia calls!' montage allow Pudovkin to advance the argument that the Provisional Government is a throwback to the tsarist system rather than a revolutionary alternative to it. He equates the two regimes by the parallels in the two sequences. The comparison is sustained by Kerensky's announcement to his audience that the Provisonal Government would continue Russia's war effort and 'bring the war to a victorious conclusion'. The tsarist regime sends men off to war, and the Provisional Government keeps them there. The bourgeoisie celebrate the war's declaration in sequence 14, and celebrate its perpetuation in sequence 18.

Figure 13

Fittingly, Lebedev also is shown supporting the Provisional Government in sequence 18, the same figure who was identified with the tsarist war effort in earlier scenes. He appears alongside Kerensky in the second half of the sequence. Through another disorienting spatial configuration, the bourgeois spectators suddenly cease to be looking down from above. They somehow reassemble around a banquet table. Kerensky and Lebedev appear in a two-shot and are praised by their wealthy admirers through a banquet toast. The reverse-angle shots of the various admirers show them as figures of extravagant wealth and link them with various icons of decadence and material excess: glasses of wine, bunches of grapes, jewels, and even an ornate fan (Figure 13). The connection of Lebedev and Kerensky with this group, and with the group's sumptuous trappings, completes the scene's indictment of the Provisional Government. Pudovkin connects the regime to exploitative capitalism in the form of Lebedev and to a renascent aristocracy in the form of this privileged class.

Sequences 19 and 21: Revolutionary Agitation; Mutiny

Pudovkin's critique of the Provisional Government provides narrative motivation for subsequent scenes about the revolutionary movement: if the Provisional Government can be shown to have betrayed the February Revolution by reincarnating the old order, the more militant activism leading to the October Revolution takes on new justification. Those more sustained revolutionary actions are the material of the film's concluding episodes. Sequences 19 and 21 show the final stages of revolutionary organization. In the former scene, factory workers are recruited to the revolutionary cause, and in the latter episode, Russian soldiers mutiny against the Provisional Government and offer their support to the Bolsheviks.

Sequence 19 at the factory opens with a jarring transition from the Kerensky banquet scene. The last image of the banquet shows a wealthy woman in jewels and fine evening attire, drinking wine while holding a particularly ornate fan. From this luxurious image, Pudovkin cuts directly to a shot of a factory smokestack. The massive, monolithic form of the stack consumes much of the frame's left half while billowing smoke obscures the sun in the frame's upper-right side. Pudovkin's cut takes us from a contrived environment, with its implications of artificial social ritual, to an image of hard, basic reality. The smokestack is a completely unadorned, functional object. Its presence implies work and productivity rather than the empty rituals of the sort on display in the Kerensky scene. This transition reiterates the shallowness of the Provisional Government's bourgeois social base and connects the Bolsheviks' worker support to a strong sense of social reality.

The scene plays out so as to sustain that impression. The Communist Worker addresses men at the Lebedev plant, urging them to support the Bolsheviks. His address counter-balances the 'performance' offered by Kerensky in the previous sequence. Whereas the Kerensky scene had the trappings of theater, this moment is rooted in the material reality of the factory world. The Communist and his worker audience appear in a series of medium shots that are framed so as to stress their hard, determined facial expressions. Often unshaven, occasionally flecked with sweat, these lined faces are meant to register the harsh effects of the industrial life. The icons of this scene are not the fineries of Kerensky's audience but the real, functional objects of the factory world, the smokestacks, power lines and industrial cranes that appear in the course of the scene. And whereas Kerensky's audience engaged in broad gestures and ostentatious displays of emotion, the workers in this scene remain virtually motionless. They are shown as an array of stern, serious faces, conveying a quiet resolve. In fact, when the Communist Worker finishes his speech with the line 'All power to the Soviets!' – a slogan that answers both 'Mother Russia calls!' and 'Long Live the Provisional Government!' – the men unite to his call, but not with animated gestures. They simply raise their right arms in solidarity. Pudovkin then promptly cuts away to shots of factory whistles blowing, giving off massive blasts of steam that fill the frame. The energy of the whistle blasts substitutes for broad movements on the part of the workers, but the whistles are none the less calculated to convey the workers' enthusiasm. They have already been used in the sequence of the February Revolution to show worker support for revolution (sequence 17). Also, in the strike scene early in the film (sequence 7), Pudovkin had shown a connection between the workers and their machines when the machines stopped on cue. Here he again connects the men to their factory environment by having the whistles express their revolutionary sentiment.

Sequence 19 also compares with the earlier strike in that the Communist Worker confronts the factory manager in a replay of a similar face-off in sequence 7. This time, however, the staging of the confrontation is different, suggesting the enhanced power of the Communist and his fellow workers. Recall that the first strike sequence began with the factory manager looming over the men until the Communist Worker rose up to meet him. In this later case, the Communist speaks to the workers in the factory yard from a platform that elevates him slightly above them. The factory manager must push awkwardly through the crowd to confront the Communist Worker. He scrambles onto the platform to denounce the Communist's agitation. But then in a brief scuffle, the Communist Worker pushes him off the platform, and he is quickly spirited away through the mass of men in the factory yard. The staging of this scene is designed to assign physical authority to the Communist Worker instead of the factory manager. Pudovkin's framing makes the Communist dominate the space, not the diminutive factory manager, who actually seems to have shrunk in size from earlier scenes. The manager is easily brushed aside as a nuisance rather than a real threat in this scene. The Communist and his worker compatriots exercise a sense of command over the factory environment in this sequence, even to the extent that the factory whistles blow on cue to express their solidarity. Pudovkin uses this staging to give graphic form to their new strength. As we will see, Pudovkin will reapply the notion of control over one's environment in later sequences as a sign of enhanced power.

The mutiny in sequence 21 is also staged so as to represent the transfer of power to the masses. The scene plays out at a military camp near St Petersburg, where troops have been recalled from the front to support the Provisional Government. The Communist Worker arrives to persuade the troops to switch allegiance from the government to the Bolshevik cause. (Recall the signs of the soldiers' discontent at the end of the war episodes.) The Communist confronts the commander – a variant of his earlier encounter with the plant manager – and then addresses the men, calling on them to rebel against their officers and join the proletarian revolution. He is joined at the head of the ranks by the Lad. When an officer orders a squad to fire on the Communist and the Lad, they direct fire at the officers instead, and the mutiny is on.

The mutiny scene is laid out so as to employ classical editing devices, but it also effects twists on the norms of continuity editing. Generally, the scene's editing follows the 180-degree rule. The ranks of soldiers are positioned on the frame's left side, and they face to the right, their collective glance falling on some space offscreen right. That space is occupied by the Communist, the Lad, and the officers, all of whom look back left when they address the soldiers. The eyelines and reverse-angle cuts keep these two groups consistently separated. But the exact locations of the officers, the Lad and the Communist at the head of the ranks remain unclear. Their glance directions are inconsistent, and Pudovkin uses no master shots to sort out their locations. This allows the dramatic turn at the scene's climax; the firing squad appears to be aiming at the Lad and the Communist but actually opens fire on the commander. Pudovkin also intentionally crosses the 180-degree line when the men actually shoot; the line of rifles points to the right in one image and to the left an instant later. Through this break in continuity, Pudovkin makes it seem that the men fire at the officer from both sides simultaneously. The mutiny achieves much of its dramatic power through these calculated violations of continuity.

The moment also contains several ingredients that highlight the shift in power toward the proletariat. When the Communist addresses the ranks of men, there is a substantial shift in shot scale between images of the Communist and shots of the soldiers. This recalls the uneven scale of Lebedev and the brokers, in which one still, solid body is measured against a larger collection of men. By replaying that configuration in the mutiny scene, Pudovkin puts the Communist in Lebedev's place, as it were, in that his authority is felt by a larger group. But it is significant that the new sense of strength emanates from a proletarian rather than a capitalist. (Lebedev disappears from the film after sequence 19.)

When the Lad joins the Communist at the head of the ranks, this gesture of solidarity signals a major stage in the Lad's development toward political awareness. He follows the mentoring lead of the Communist in encouraging the soldiers' rebellion – literally breaking ranks to do so – and when he goes to the head of the rank, he even assumes the same pose as that of the Communist (Figure 14). His gesture of determination contrasts with his earlier desultory behavior. His body language changes accordingly, from the slow, heavy movements of earlier scenes to this

Figure 14

decisive action. This marks the end of his association with the lumpen sensibility. The Lad's growth derives from an enhanced political consciousness that will motivate his activism in the film's final scenes.

Sequence 20: Husband's Escape

Sequences 19 and 21 parallel each other by showing growing support for Bolshevism among both workers and soldiers. Those two episodes flank the crucial scene at the Wife's apartment in which she helps her husband escape from the police (sequence 20). That scene motivates the Wife's final commitment to the Bolshevik cause. It thus complements the two scenes that bracket it: whereas they both show groups of men recruited to the cause, this scene shows a woman acting as an individual and making an equivalent commitment. It marks her final moment of political education and thus parallels the epiphany that her counterpart character, the Lad, experiences in sequence 21.

This scene opens as the Communist Worker returns home at night after an extended absence. The Wife greets him and prepares to serve him tea. He soon steps out for tobacco, and while he is gone police arrive hoping to arrest him and then lie in wait. When he returns, the Wife sees him outside and throws the teacup through the window to warn him. He escapes as a result, but she is arrested. A set of titles invoking 'Freedom, EQUALITY!, BROTHERHOOD!' (emphasis in original) appears on screen when she is arrested.

This scene is shot in an economical continuity style, the most rigorous such example in the entire film.[8] The style's application in this case maintains a close viewer identity with the character of the Wife. It renders her experience of the moment in vivid form, and provides the audience with an understanding of her growing awareness of social injustice. Pudovkin achieves this by making her the scene's point-of-view character; through a series of glances and reactions, including nuanced applications of the Kuleshov effect, audience members take in the scene through her perception of it. Her response is then supposed to be felt all the more strongly by audience members because of the scene's confined point-of-view.[9]

For example, certain devices in this episode put the Wife's feelings on display. In the scene's opening, she sits alone at the table and seems to drift off to sleep. Pudovkin inserts shots of a clock and a wick lamp to mark the passage of time. These objects are not assigned a specific location in the apartment; they were never shown in any previous episode at the flat and no establishing shot in this scene indicates where they might reside. They appear more-or-less as projections of her growing sensation of sleepiness. The clock, for example, is not shown on the wall; rather it is framed with a darkened background that does not fit the lighting of the scene. It has a pendulum swinging in a steady rhythm that would indicate a monotonous but hypnotic ticking noise, the sound the Wife would experience as she drifted off. Thus the clock's sound, rather than its location is privileged, evoking the Wife's psychological experience of that sound. Later when her husband steps out, Pudovkin reuses these clock and lamp images to reiterate her feeling of time passing. The clock comes back when the police wait in ambush for the husband's return; in this case it becomes a projection of the Wife's growing unease over the prospect of her husband's arrest. Pudovkin uses it one last time when the husband is pursued down the street by police. In this instance, it manifests the Wife's tense uncertainty over whether her husband can escape. These motifs thus take us through her range of emotions as the scene plays out.

Otherwise, Pudovkin uses glances to illustrate the Wife's reactions to what happens around her. She awakens after the scene's opening passage when she hears a sound outside in the street, which happens to be her husband walking home. When she wakes up, she glances up at the window that faces on to the street, and then she turns and looks at the apartment door. These glances indicate that she is responding to a sound (at the window), that she anticipates her husband's return (at the door). It also informs us where the window and door are located and that she can hear sounds from outside, information that will figure later in the geography of the escape. When the Communist Worker then steps out for tobacco, he pauses outside the window. The Wife looks back up at the window, and a point-of-view shot reveals that she can see him through the glass. When the police enter the apartment during the husband's absence, she is alerted to their intrusion when the lamp flame flickers, Pudovkin's visual indicator that a breeze has passed through the room because the door has opened. The Wife responds to the sensation of the wind by turning, looking toward the door (the wind's source) and then shrinking back in apparent fear. A reverse angle shows the police standing in the doorway. Her cringing reaction was to their unwelcome presence. On the occasion of both her husband's return and the intrusion of the police, the glances reveal her to be responding to immediate physical phenomena, in the one case to sound and in the other case to the feel of a breeze. Thus, even her physiological sensations are put on display.

The series of glances at the teacup on the table shifts attention from her feelings to her thoughts. The husband's tea serving remains on the table while he goes out for tobacco. Its presence provides a clue to the police that the husband must be nearby. A long shot shows a policeman on the left of the frame, the table (with the cup visible) in the center, and the Wife on the right. This provides an establishing shot and a 180-degree axis for subsequent close shots. Pudovkin then shows a series of reverse-angle profiles of the policeman looking offscreen right and the Wife looking back toward the left. The exchanges conform to the 180-degree rule and thus provide a consistent sense of space in which the tea is between the two antagonists. Pudovkin duly inserts a close-up of the cup into this exchange; that insert clearly shows steam emanating from the hot tea. The two characters in this encounter thus take turns glancing at the cup and at each other. Several quick Kuleshov-like combinations reveal what they are thinking. The police inspector surmises from the cup's presence and from the steam it still gives off that the husband has stepped out, but probably not for long. He decides to wait. The Wife reacts to the policeman's expression and to his decision to wait. She calculates that the husband's proximity is betrayed and that he will be trapped. That knowledge motivates her decision to help him a few moments later when he escapes, but first that knowledge is confirmed through the reverse-angle glances and reactions.

Pudovkin uses consistent screen direction again for the husband's escape. The husband pauses on the street by the window on his way home. The Wife glances up and left from her position by the table in a way that has already been carefully set up as the direction of the window. Quick point-of-view shots follow, which confirm that the Wife sees him outside. She then grabs the cup in a long shot and throws it in the same direction as her glance, that is toward the window. Pudovkin cuts on a match on action of the throw. The reverse-angle shot of the cup hitting the window follows the direction of her previous point-of-view shot. The directional cues of her glance are thus exactly matched in her action of throwing the cup. This spatial economy confirms that the husband has been alerted and will make his escape.

We have seen elsewhere that Pudovkin can purposely create false or misleading spatial relations, sometimes by using classical editing devices. In this scene, the continuity devices are employed to develop a precise, coherent dramatic space. The scene involves a tense drama played out in a small space; in fact, the drama is intensified precisely by the fact that it is so contained. And those confines help the audience focus closely on the Wife's reactions. The same continuity devices that articulate a confined space for the actions also magnify the Wife's response to those actions. Pudovkin stages the scene so as to display both her feelings and her thoughts. We thus become aware of what would motivate her to risk herself, as well as the political lesson she learns from taking that risk.

The film's narrative form commonly matches specific personal incidents with passages that generalize from those incidents. The Wife's experience in the escape scene provides a case study of personal response to political inequity: in other words, these are the specific feelings and thoughts someone might have when confronting injustice. Its generalizing counterpart does not appear in an adjacent scene in this case, but in the scene's own conclusion. The final titles declaring 'Freedom, EQUALITY!, BROTHERHOOD!' involve an extrapolation from the specific incident to an understanding of its larger meaning, broad concepts drawn out of the individual case. They express the Wife's now fully developed political consciousness, as she recognizes that such ideals now must supplant her earlier, narrow views about personal survival. She does not, in fact, utter those words. They appear in expository rather than dialogue titles, an outside voice that comments on the lesson of her arrest in a broad, rhetorical gesture equivalent to 'What are we dying for?' in the war scene. The titles provide the larger lesson for the spectator to take from this incident.

In terms of the Wife's development, that lesson marks the end of her political development. It provides the final motivation for her commitment to the revolutionary cause, and explains her presence at the

Winter Palace in the film's last scene. And fittingly, the incident that pushes her to this level of commitment involves political injustice in the home. In the film's early stages, the Wife tried to maintain that home as a sanctuary for her family, to keep her and the children safe from the political turmoil of the outside. That sense of sanctuary gradually breaks down as outsiders violate the space, from the Lad (sequence 6), to the strikers (sequence 8), to the authorities (sequences 9, 21). Meanwhile, as noted earlier, the Wife ventures out and participates in that external political reality. Part of the lesson of the incident in the escape sequence is that those two realms – private and public, domestic and political, inside and outside – are not mutually exclusive. Political injustice impinges on the private life, literally entering the home in this case. The response involves a recognition of the connection between private well-being and political activism. That connection is made evident in her action. When the Wife throws the cup through the window, the gesture is fully motivated as her pragmatic response to an emergency in the home. Fittingly, it involves a domestic object, a teacup. She first serves her husband the tea with a touching sense of domestic tenderness. But she then transforms the cup from being a domestic item into something of a political weapon, a way to strike out against oppression. Her gesture of throwing it through the window and smashing the glass also recalls images from the February Revolution when women are shown throwing stones through shop windows (sequence 17), thus associating the political activism of the street with an act of home defense. And in saving her husband, she aids both her domestic partner – and this scene contains the first moments of tenderness between them – and her political mentor. Her character's growth illustrates the connection between those realms.

Sequence 22: Assault on the Winter Palace

The final two sequences of *The End of St Petersburg* are set at the Winter Palace and its environs. Both the narrative climax (sequence 22) and denouement (sequence 23) take advantage of that location. Of course, one would expect the Winter Palace assault to be re-created in a film commemorating the October Revolution. Although the actual 25 October attack was decidedly second-rate as battles go, it had enormous symbolic significance as a revolutionary act and was duly celebrated in Soviet lore. The symbolic quality of the event doubtless had much to do with the palace itself, the largest and most luxurious of St Petersburg's many imperial buildings. This extravagant, baroque edifice was the bastion of tsarism and of Russia's elites. That common workers and soldiers, in their rough, utilitarian attire, could come in off the streets and take possession of the ornate palace seemed to signal a whole new social order.

Pudovkin gives particular attention to the symbolic weight of the location in the film's final two sequences. His rendering of the assault in sequence 22 offers only a fragmentary, abbreviated account of the military logistics of the action. Instead, he emphasizes the physical environment itself, the palace grounds. And in the final scene on the morning after, he portrays the working class's new control of that environment. This contributes to the theme of the gradual habilitation of the proletariat, including the film's central characters. One sign of that enhanced power is their growing command of their environment, including control of a location from which they were previously barred.

The montage of the assault sequence spends more time on the details of the Winter Palace than it does illustrating the attack. Consider the following passage from the beginning of the attack sequence: (1) Two armed Red Guards, poised to attack, look offscreen right; (2) One Red Guard looks off right; (3) Medium shot of palace gate, viewed from left; (4) Long shot of palace façade, viewed from left; (5) Palace balustrade, viewed from lower left; (6) A row of palace statues of human figures, seeming to look off left; (7) Close shot of Red Guard, looking back right.

This array balances shots of people with images of objects from the locale. Shots of Red Guard troops (shots 1, 2, 7) are matched with architectural details from the palace grounds (shots 3–6) in a tidy symmetry. The directions of soldiers' glances match the direction from which the palace details are seen. In one exchange, the statues on the building's façade face to the left (shot 6), and the next shot shows a soldier looking back right (shot 7) as though the man and the statues actually exchange glances in matched eyelines.

Such editing patterns make the palace grounds, not the opposition forces, the objective of the attack. The sequence virtually ignores the palace defenders and does not show any representatives of the Provisional Government (who were actually barricaded in the building on 25 October). The editing instead stresses the building's ornate details (statues, façade, decorations on the gate), and it seems to pit Bolshevik soldiers against the details of the palace, not against opposition forces. This idea is reiterated by the repeated intertitle 'Against the Winter Palace' (not 'Against the Provisional Government').

This staging makes the 'conquering' of a space, the palace grounds, a sign of the proletariat's new power. Recall that earlier in the film, the workers effectively took command of the factory location: an environment that had once oppressed them (sequence 3) was transformed into a space that they came to dominate (sequence 19). Now, in sequence 22, their authority spreads out to an area that had previously not been within their ken or control, the palace grounds. The proletariat's space at the start of the film was limited to a few locales: the factory, the tenement district, the Wife's apartment. But their area of authority grows in the film's second half. The demonstrations of the February Revolution constituted one such act to extend the domain of the working class, as proletarian women (including the Wife) ventured out to take command of the streets. That action by working-class women in sequence 17 is balanced by working-class men who take over the palace district in sequence 22.

In seizing the Winter Palace, they control one of St Petersburg's imperialist landmarks, and this fits into another of the film's motific patterns. Starting with Lad's arrival in St Petersburg in sequence 2, Pudovkin periodically inserts images of monuments or public buildings as signs of the imperial heritage. Typically, such landmarks are filmed so as to emphasize either their size or grandeur. Recall, for example, that certain famous statues, such as the Bronze Horseman, were initially depicted as great, overwhelming objects. By the film's end, however, such objects are depicted in an different scale. They are brought down to more human dimensions. In fact, in sequence 22, they start to *resemble* humans rather than looming up over them as powerful objects. As noted above, reverse-angle edits sometimes make the statues seem to exchange glances with soldiers involved in the assault. The poses of some Winter Palace statues even occasionally seem to match those of the men. For example, the Lad's stance and offscreen stare in one shot finds its equivalent in the statue profiles a few shots later. Also a shot of the Bronze Horseman is inserted into the assault scene, showing Peter the Great with his arm extended. That pose is answered at the end of the assault sequence when the Communist Worker is shown in silhouette with his arm raised. This gesture by the Communist signals the success of the assault, that the palace has fallen to the Red Guards. It is also an image of power, and the reference to Peter the Great in the matched poses extends the implications of that gesture, to indicate that power has shifted from the forces of imperialism to the proletariat. By diminishing the iconography of the old guard, Pudovkin enhances the sense of authority of the working class.

If the Provisional Government is absent from the assault sequence, so is the Bolshevik leadership. The sequence does not show Party leaders organizing the attack; nor does it show the command structure of the Red Guard assault forces. Expository titles indicate how the attack was co-ordinated – the approach of the cruiser *Aurora*, the volley from the Peter and Paul Fortress – but we do not see commanders or Party officials making plans and issuing orders. Pudovkin's purposeful omission of the Bolsheviks' command echelon fits his pattern in *The End of St Petersburg* of measuring the revolutionary experience from the bottom up rather than from the top down. He has left the Party leaders out of the rest of the film, and he specifically omits them from association with the Bolshevik Revolution's single most storied event, the Winter Palace assault. The effect of that omission in the assault sequence is to imply that the common troops somehow prevail through their own skill and revolutionary élan. They do not require commanders, so strong is their commitment to the cause. By the start of the assault sequence, Pudovkin has already offered models of how common citizens acquire such revolutionary consciousness and solidarity. That transfers to the men involved in the assault. They can now proceed to make a political revolution based on these newly acquired revolutionary attributes.

While Pudovkin omits Bolshevik leaders from sequence 23, he makes a point of including the Communist Worker and the Lad. These two common-man heroes are duly shown to be among the assault troops. It is appropriate in the narrative economy of the film that the two figures should appear in the climatic scene, given how they have been linked throughout the film. The Communist Worker has led by example, and mentored those around him, including the Lad, in revolutionary politics. The Lad has grown into that consciousness, in substantial measure because of the Communist Worker's model. Their connection as representatives of an enlightened proletariat was confirmed at the end of sequence 21 when the two stood together and led the army mutiny. They carry that new parallel identity over into the next sequence, the Winter Palace attack. In fact, it is the Lad who fires the assault's opening volley, and the Communist who signals the attack's success with his triumphant gesture of the raised arm. Their presence among the assault forces provides us with a narrative rationale for assuming that other Red Guard troops have gone through similar political educations and are thus prepared to press forward on their own in the name of revolution. Pudovkin's specific/general dynamic thus operates again in this scene. He places a central character in a larger group, and encourages us to extrapolate the specific lessons of his experience to that general population. As the central characters have grown and become active, so has the larger proletarian mass around them.

Sequence 23: Morning After

The final sequence of *The End of St Petersburg* serves several functions. It draws together and concludes various motifs having to do with the theme of empowerment. And it brings together the three central characters for a final episode of reconciliation and unity. In so doing the sequence hints at the more egalitarian society the characters might expect to inhabit in the communist future.

Sequence 23 is best described as offering a sense of calm. The film built to a dramatic climax through the ascending emotional arc of the prior three scenes, the escape, the mutiny and, of course, the storming of the Winter Palace (sequences 20–22). The final episode then provides a quiet denouement to offset those conflicts and to measure their outcomes. As it happens, the morning after the actual 25 October coup was tranquil compared to the turmoil of the previous days. As the scene plays out in the film, its relaxed quality derives from the absence of narrative conflict, which conflicts were resolved in the prior climatic scenes. The conflict-free narrative condition of sequence 23 translates into an image of a society free of discord. The implication is that the class conflicts invoked in the course of the narrative have been effectively resolved by revolution in favor of a more harmonious social order. The calm ease with which soldiers and civilians occupy the palace grounds enhances this sense of casual harmony. The tender aid that these revolutionaries offer to wounded comrades adds to the impression of brotherhood.[10]

This image of social harmony takes more specific form in the moments of reconciliation between the three central characters. As he has done throughout the film, Pudovkin matches a large-scale societal situation with its specific application to individual citizens. In this case, the three central characters, who represent a social cross-section, display amity toward one another. Their interactions provide the personal microcosm of the larger social accord. Sequence 23 is only the second time in the film that all three central characters appear together in the same scene. The first came in the confrontation in the apartment (sequence 8), in a scene which illustrated the socio-economic problems that divided them and created friction. In this final sequence, it is appropriate that Pudovkin should stage a reconciliation to indicate how those problems have been resolved through the communist revolution.

The reconciliation between the Wife and the Lad is staged to have an especially poignant tone. And once again, continuity devices take over for this intimate exchange between the two characters, with glances and reaction shots serving to define the emotions of the moment. The Wife goes to the palace grounds looking for her husband. She carries a small

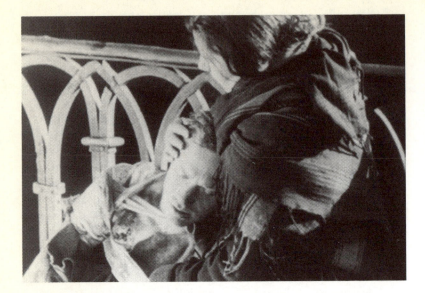

Figure 15

pail containing potatoes. Outside the palace, she pauses near several Red Guards, some of whom are resting and some of whom are wounded. She is asked to assist a wounded man who lies with his back to the camera, delaying for the moment the revelation of his identity. She walks over to him and kneels down. In a reverse-angle close-up, he turns to look back up at her and is revealed to be the Lad. Another reverse angle yields a close-up of the Wife's face as she recognizes him. Tears are visible in her eyes. The next reverse angle to his face indicates that he now recognizes her, and he offers a tender smile mixed with the pain he feels from his wounds. In a tight close-up of her, she moves down to embrace him. Then a two-shot shows her cradling him in her arms (Figure 15).

Pudovkin has used continuity for small personal exchanges throughout the film. In this most emotionally charged of encounters, he strives for particular intimacy in these eyeline exchanges, using the tightest framings of the film. When the Lad turns and the two characters recognize each other, their mutual emotions are put on full display in these extreme close-ups. They are seeing each other for the first time since their tense confrontations in the apartment. The harshness of those earlier meetings is countered by the tenderness of this one. And it is worth recalling that the narrative provides no interpersonal motivation for the reconciliation of these two characters; there are no intermediate scenes showing them gradually getting to like each other, for example. The reconciliation is done suddenly in this denouement, leaving us to understand that an outside force must explain it, namely the new forms of harmony made possible by a communist revolution.

The comparison of this moment with the apartment confrontations indicates how far the characters have come. Their emotional expressions, especially the Wife's tears, contrast with the deadened attitudes they displayed in the earlier apartment scenes. The Wife appeared as the jaded product of a harsh environment when first seen. The Lad seemed aimless and abject. Now they both appear as emotionally enriched and capable of true compassion. Their political education and their participation in selfless activism seem to have helped produce this new sense of empathy. If the old tsarist regime had left the characters stunted, the new order promises to sustain fuller emotional development. Once again, Pudovkin reminds us that the revolution benefits not just an economic class, but it also serves to enhance personal lives.

The Wife's gesture of cradling the Lad's head reinforces that suggestion. The gesture alludes to the maternal pose the Wife struck in sequence 8 when she held her baby (see Figures 10 and 15). By repeating it in the last sequence, Pudovkin summons up several associations. It reinforces the idea of a new brand of empathy that can cut across societal categories: an urban woman treats a representative of the peasantry as though he is one of her own children. It also suggests a new, extended definition of family: not just immediate relatives but fellow members of the laboring classes. This conceit is sustained by the fact that when the Wife first used the gesture, she was in the confines of the home, a space reserved for the protection and sustenance of the immediate family. But when she repeats it, she is in a public space, the palace grounds, in a locale that is now associated with proletarian triumph. And on this second occasion she is surrounded, not by relatives, but by an array of proletarians. A gesture initially reserved for her family is now shared with representatives of an entire social class.

The potato motif completes this connection between the domestic and public spheres. When the Wife sees the various wounded and tired soldiers at the palace grounds, she offers them the potatoes she had brought along in the pail. Then she walks over to the Lad and gives him the last of the container's contents. When she finally leaves this group to enter the Winter Palace, she carries an empty pail. Since she came to the palace grounds to search for her husband, one can assume that she meant the potatoes for him. After all, we have seen that potatoes constitute the family's staple diet. When she finally meets her husband inside the Winter Palace, he notes that the pail is empty. This provokes a gentle smile, not a rebuke over the missing foodstuffs. Those victuals went not to this member of her nuclear family (and he does not seem to mind), but to her larger, metaphorical 'family' of proletarians. Whereas she had formerly hoarded these items as private possessions, they now become public property. It is especially fitting that she should offer the last of the potatoes to the Lad, since she previously refused to feed him (sequence 6). By returning one last time to this motif, Pudovkin allows us to measure the characters' considerable growth and development since their first such encounter.

The moment when the Wife meets the Communist Worker inside the Winter Palace complements her encounter with the Lad outside and completes the scene's cycle of interpersonal connections. The Wife and her husband meet at the top of the palace's Jordan Staircase where they exchange smiles with a tenderness and mutual pleasure that would have been impossible in the early, tense scenes back in their apartment. We are left to understand that the success of the revolution, and the path the two characters took toward that revolution, brought these spouses to a condition of mutual respect and affection, something they were unable to achieve under the oppressive conditions of the old order. The personal benefits of revolution are thus shown to extend to marital relations.

The location of this encounter is significant as well. The Winter Palace district contrasts with the workers' spartan tenement district. The palace setting permits a freedom of movement, as opposed to the impression of enclosure in the tenements. And the palace's interior is spacious, bright and ornate, a far cry from the cold, dank environment of the Wife's apartment.

That sense of freedom is manifested in the Wife's walk through the palace hallway and up the Jordan Staircase. The moment receives particular attention in a series of tracking and panning shots: (1) After she enters the building, she walks along the corridor toward the stairs. The camera follows her in a graceful tracking shot. Palace columns and stacks of rifles on either side of the corridor slide past the camera; (2) Cut to a second tracking shot, now closer to the stairs. This is from the Wife's point-of-view; (3) Long shot of her beginning to ascend stairs; (4) Point-of-view shot of ornamentation in stairwell; (5) Point-of-view shot of ceiling ornamentation; (6) Long shot of her ascending steps; (7) Panning point-of-view shot of ornamentation in stairwell; (8) Long shot of Wife ascending steps; (9) Close-up of empty pail; (10) Panning point-of-view shot of stairwell; (11) Superimposed images of stairwell details.

The narrative rationale for the passage is simply to get the Wife into the Winter Palace to meet her husband, who happens to be standing at the top of the stairs. Pudovkin intentionally over-elaborates this process, however, taking eleven shots to get her up the steps. He protracts the action in order to stress the spectacular qualities of the setting and to celebrate the triumphal experience of moving through that space. This woman who was initially confined to a dingy flat can now walk through this extravagant building and take in its splendor. The several point-of-view shots in the passage re-create for the spectator the feeling of exhilaration that such an experience would offer. This is emphasized by the fact that Pudovkin chooses to use both tracks (shots 1, 2) and pans (shots 8, 10) to provide a feeling of actually *moving* through this space.

The choice of traveling shots for this passage is significant. For one thing, this particular interior was designed to offer the palace's privileged inhabitants a dazzling visual experience while walking along the corridor and up the stairs. In fact, the space is designed to be taken in while moving. The columns and Rococo decorations are positioned to flow gracefully past when one walks through the area and to offer a shifting matrix of sights. Historically, this visual sensation was offered only to monarchs and to the nobility. Pudovkin makes a point of celebrating the fact that a simple working-class woman now has that experience available to her. (There is even a slightly ironic proletarian touch in the passage's first shot. Stacks of rifles, left behind by Red Guards, line the corridor in a configuration that matches the columns.) The flowing sensation of the moving and point-of-view shots renders her sense of wonder at the moment and shares that wonder with the audience. The passage even ends with a welter of superimposed images of the Wife's surroundings (shot 11), as though she is overwhelmed by the sights which start to run together in her mind.

It is also worth noting that, with the exception of brief traveling shots in sequence 2, these pans and tracks are the only moving-camera shots of the entire film. As noted, Pudovkin's stylistic parameters throughout the film involve the alternatives of continuity editing and open-ended montage. Pudovkin generally eschews long takes or mobile shots. But he has saved that option to use at this particular moment. The moving camera functions to provide a feeling of graceful flow as the Wife passes through that environment. It also offers a feeling of freedom. She can move about at will in a world that would once have been off-limits to her and to members of her class. In this respect, the moment contributes to the film's theme of proletarian entitlement. The extent to which representatives of that class gain control of the space around them has provided a pattern to measure this. As noted, acquisition of the Winter Palace marks the culmination of that motif. In the theme's specific application to the Wife, we have seen her progress from the confines of the flat (sequence 6) and out to the streets (sequence 17) earlier in the film. The ease with which she passes through the spacious Winter Palace grounds – emphasized through Pudovkin's graceful traveling shots – completes the pattern of her expanded freedom of movement.

Not only do proletarians exercise direct, physical control over new locales by the film's end; they also experience expanded authority through commanding glances. As noted earlier, various of St Petersburg's monuments and cityscapes gradually change character, from seeming to be overwhelming and oppressive (sequence 2) to appearing more human and accessible (sequence 22). Changes in shot scale, especially in point-of-view shots, effect this shift. As these glance-objects diminish in scale, the relative power of the point-of-view characters seems to increase. Recall how the Lad was subordinated to the imperial monuments he encountered early in the film. In the final scene, the Wife can look upon the Winter Palace, the bastion of tsarist power, with a sense of ownership. When she prepares to enter the palace, for example, she pauses to look at its façade. The spatial relations between shots of her glance and shots of the palace façade do not subordinate her. The framing does not depict her as a tiny person looking at something huge, but as someone of sizable stature herself. Her profile fills the screen, balancing the image of the building's façade. This new pattern in point-of-view framings connotes the increased power and extended ken of these representatives of the proletariat. As they begin to exert more authority over their world, their view of that world is duly enhanced. As their knowledge of the world grows through political education, so does their visual ken.

That theme is carefully worked out in the course of the film through Pudovkin's measured shifts in framing and shot scale. It takes a hyperbolic turn, however, in the film's final moments. When the Wife and her husband meet at the top of the stairs and exchange smiles, intertitles declare 'Long Live the City of Lenin!' They are followed by the film's very last shot which shows the Communist Worker smiling, not so much down at his Wife on the stairs, but out at the camera and thus at the audience. This proclamation and the Communist Worker's expression are offered to end the film on a celebratory note, and to direct it at the audience. The anachronistic nature of the remark has already been noted: the city would only be renamed some years later under the Soviet regime. That anachronism is intentional, as was the decision to use the name St Petersburg instead of Petrograd throughout the film. Elsewhere the sequence contains the declaration that 'St Petersburg is no more', meaning that the old order, best identified in the city's original name, has been brought down by revolution. The St Peterburg appellation is used to evoke the past; the Lenin eponym, then, is to invoke the future, the city's later incarnation under the Soviets. And the declaration about the 'City of Lenin' in the final intertitle is linked to the Communist Worker, the character whose communist wisdom always allows him to foresee developments. (Recall how he counseled others based on his advanced knowledge.) In this instance, his knowledge projects into the future, as though he knows that this city will eventually carry Lenin's name. In fact, he seems almost to *see* into the future; his glance at the end is not down at his Wife, but outward. There is no object of his glance in a follow-up shot, no conventional eyeline match. In an overextended metaphor, Pudovkin makes the *future* the object of the character's glance, as though the Communist's extended ken includes the ability to see where history is heading.

Recall that Pudovkin and Zarkhi reduced the scope of the film's narrative in script development. They cut out material on how St Petersburg (Leningrad) changed under the Soviets. This final sequence compensates by condensing into the first morning after the Bolshevik Revolution – the first morning of communism, as it were – various suggestions of the better world to come. And morning is an appropriate setting for such utopian projections, since morning is associated with optimistic tropes about the possibilities of a 'new day'. The film thus ends with an promising 'glance' into the future; and by associating Lenin's name with things to come, Pudovkin links that future with the promised benefits of communism.

At least one such benefit, Pudovkin suggests, is the empowerment of the individual, as evidenced by the enhanced ken of the central characters at the film's conclusion. In fact this constitutes the culmination of what has been the central theme of *The End of St Petersburg*. Pudovkin's main characters, especially the Lad and the Wife, gradually acquired the knowledge and sophistication to participate in change. But they were also each strengthened by that change. They ceased to be victims of a political system they could not control and became makers of a new political system that will benefit them.

Pudovkin used his strategic pattern of alternating between the classical style and the montage style to measure this shifting power relationship between society and the individual. And his shifts in narrative scale, between mass scenes and intimate episodes, keep us apprised of the characters' developmental progress as they reshape historical events.

When most Western scholars comment on Soviet silent cinema, certain characterizations come forward immediately: radical editing practices, mass heroes instead of individual protagonists, collectivist ideologies. Pudovkin's work may not belie those common characterizations, but he demonstrates the possible benefits of more multidimensional descriptions. *The End of St Petersburg* borrows from more than one stylistic and narrative tradition, and puts forward a historical account of revolution that takes account of *both* the individual and the mass. The film matches perfectly conventional editing with avant-garde devices. It give us nuanced, psychologically defined characters along with mass scenes of epic events. And to Pudovkin's everlasting credit, he argues that the ultimate reward of a collectivist system is, finally, its benefits to the collective's individual members.

Notes

1. Katerina Clark, *The Soviet Novel: History as Ritual*, Chicago, IL, 1985, ch. 2.
2. This shifting sense of story time in *The End of St Petersburg* is discussed in Pierre Sorlin's account of the film in *The Film in History*, London, 1980, pp. 167–9.
3. See Amy Sargeant, *Vsevolod Pudovkin: Classic Films of the Soviet Avant-Garde*, London and New York, 2000, pp. 93–4.
4. This image takes a familiar religious motif and recasts it as a secular image supporting a left revolutionary theme. Interestingly, the characters in the film show no religious conviction, even during the pre-revolutionary episodes of the story. The church is not in evidence in the village scene (sequence 1). There is no religious iconography in the Wife's apartment or any wall decorations of any kind. Since the husband is identified in the film as a communist sympathizer, one can understand that religion would not figure in the family's existence. Also, the production design of the apartment calls for a stark coldness. This is served by barren, gray walls and would be undercut by the presence of icons or any decorative touches.
5. See V. I. Lenin, *Imperialism: The Highest Stage of Capitalism* (13th edn), Moscow, 1966.
6. Anatoli Golovnya, 'Broken Cudgels', in Luda and Jean Schnitzer and Marcel Martin (eds), *Cinema in Revolution*, trans. David Robinson, New York, 1973, p. 141.
7. It bears a resemblance to the 'God and Country' sequence of Eisenstein's *October* and may provide further evidence of Eisenstein's influence on *The End of St Petersburg*.
8. I have tried to describe in greater detail the scene's use of continuity devices to develop a tight dramatic space: Kepley, 'Pudovkin and the Continuity Style: Problems of Space and Narration', *Discourse*, 17, no. 3 (1995), pp. 85–100. See also Sergei Tretiakov's admiring comments on the scene's narrative

economy, quoted in Jay Leyda, *Kino: A History of the Russian and Soviet Film* (3rd edn), Princeton, NJ, 1983, pp. 236–7.

9. One can find the equivalent strategy at work in the trial scene of Pudovkin's *The Mother*. In that scene, the title character (also played by Vera Baranov-skaia) sits in the spectators' gallery as her son is tried for subversion. By making her a spectator at the proceedings and by using glances and reaction shots, Pudovkin privileges her perception of the event. She experiences a similar recognition of injustice at the end of that scene.

10. On this impression of tranquility and its ideological implications, see Pan-ayiota Mini, 'Pudovkin's Cinema of the 1920s', PhD dissertation, University of Wisconsin-Madison, 2002, pp. 294–6.

4. After-effects

We have seen that a network of interdependent historical circumstances from the 1920s helped shape *The End of St Petersburg*. Changing conditions played an equally important role in the film's subsequent career, helping to determine how it would be received and the place it would hold in the annals of Soviet cinema. To account for these matters, I will look into the film's immediate release, its effect on the subsequent course of Pudovkin's career, and the problem *The End of St Petersburg* has posed in assessing that career. And in treating these issues, I will return to what has been a central concern of this study, the film's diverse ingredients. The hybrid design of *The End of St Petersburg* affected its immediate reception and its longer-term standing in the cinema canon. An evolving intellectual environment defined and then redefined the terms under which *The End of St Petersburg* and Pudovkin's work generally could be appreciated.

Immediate Reception

The film's public career began in November 1927 when *The End of St Petersburg* was readied for preview. Pudovkin rushed the film through the final stages of production to have it available by 7 November, the anniversary of the Winter Palace assault (new-style calendar) and the official date of the Jubilee celebration. Pudovkin realized his deadline, and submitted the film for a special Jubilee performance at Moscow's Bolshoi Theater. There it played in conjunction with another anniversary film, Barnet's *Moscow in October*. Shub's documentary feature *The Great Road* premièred the day before as part of the celebration. Only a few sections of Eisenstein's *October* were available for preview by November 1927, and its release date had to be delayed until the following March.[1] Pudovkin's film was thus able to reap the benefit of a first wave of publicity and political good-will related to the events of the anniversary.

Mezhrabpom withheld the film from commercial distribution until mid-December, however, five weeks after the Jubilee. This might seem like bad timing, since the free publicity of the anniversary events would have worn off by the time of that release. Both *Moscow in October* and *The Great Road* went into wide distribution immediately after 7 November and cashed in on the anniversary. But Mezhrabpom wanted *The End of St Petersburg* to open in its company-owned venue, the large Moscow theater Koloss. In a dilemma that was all too characteristic of Mezhrabpom, it had to delay showing its revolutionary film so as to exploit a commercial opportunity. The German film *Variety* [Variété, 1925] was already playing there in November, and the import proved so popular that Mezhrabpom carried it over for an extended run until mid-December, thus delaying *The End of St Petersburg*'s first run until the week of 14 December.[2] The incident betrayed the company's continuing negotiation between public service and commercial considerations.

Whatever the effect of the timing of its release, *The End of St Petersburg*'s overall commercial performance proved to be weak by the standards of Mezhrabpom. *The End of St Petersburg* earned only 325,000 rubles in general distribution. By way of comparison, the studio's big commercial hits made several times that amount. Mezhrabpom's entertaining action serial *Miss Mend* [1926], for example, earned over 3.2 million rubles, and the melodrama *The Bear's Wedding* took in 829,000 rubles. *The End of St Petersburg*'s earnings even seem small in comparison with Pudovkin's other major features. Both *The Mother* and *Storm Over Asia*, the films Pudovkin made just before and after *The End of St Petersburg*, earned over half a million rubles each.[3]

The film's modest box-office receipts need not have been a point of great concern to Mezhrabpom. The studio made *The End of St Petersburg* more to accumulate political capital than box-office revenue. After all, a Pudovkin loss leader could be offset on the company's books by the next comedy or adventure movie to go into commercial distribution. By contributing an officially sanctioned film to the Soviet government's anniversary celebration, the company hoped to counter charges of 'nepism'. *The End of St Petersburg* represented for Mezhrabpom the capstone of the company's enlightenment campaign, the films the studio began producing in 1925 (e.g. *His Call*, *The Mechanics of the Brain*) to offset its reputation for commercialism. Mezhrabpom even timed a company reorganization with the distribution of *The End of St Petersburg*. The studio removed the last vestiges of its connection to the pre-revolutionary film organization Rus, which association had sustained the impression of Mezhrabpom as something of a bourgeois bastion. The company changed its official name from *Mezhrabpom-Rus'* to *Mezhrabpomfil'm* to establish a new image, and that image was to be promoted by politically enlightening films such as *The End of St Petersburg*.[4]

Company leaders may have been more concerned by the reviews *The End of St Petersburg* received in the Soviet press. They might have hoped for consistently glowing notices for a film produced and issued in the spirit of public service. But *The End of St Petersburg* had a mixed critical reception. The major official newspapers, *Pravda* and *Izvestiia*, both offered positive reviews; the latter praised *The End of St Petersburg* as 'an important artistic production, a step forward for the director and for Soviet cinema', and predicted that Pudovkin would soon 'see his name listed among the very best [film-makers], both at home and abroad'.[5]

Other reviewers were less generous. They criticized the film's complicated narrative form, claiming that it seemed fragmented and diffuse. Its various sub-plots and its episodic narrative prompted complaints that the film lacked cohesion and threatened to leave some viewers confused.[6] One of the strongest expressions of dissent came from the respected literary critic and screenwriter Victor Shklovsky, who offered an extended critique of the film's mixed style.[7] He surmised that revisions had sacrificed the narrative balance present in the parallel sub-plots of the film's earlier script versions. After cutting the counterbalancing sub-plot of the White Guard sympathizer (see Chapter 2), Pudovkin needed something to compensate: 'We are left with a plot line that unfolds the story of a worker's family. But this line is not contrasted with a different plot line; instead it is placed against a background of historical montage.'[8] The central story of the worker's family is conventional, but the montage passages seem abstract and poetic by comparison. Instead of shifting between two sub-plots with equivalent tones, Pudovkin shifts between a prosaic tone in the plot of the worker's family and a poetic tone in the montage passages. That produces an aesthetic tension throughout the work, Shklovsky concluded.

Shklovsky's comments specifically address the film's mixed-mode status. Pudovkin consciously developed a composite style in *The End of St Petersburg* that is calculated to produce internal tensions. One consequence of that decision can be measured in the film's troubled reception. Ironically, Pudovkin embraced the classical style because of its capacity for narrative clarity. And as we have seen, he sought to adapt it to the

Soviet situation in the hope that it would offer clear, precise messages to a diverse audience. But in mixing it with the montage style, he came forth with a modernist, rather than a classical work. *The End of St Petersburg* has an eclectic look that is more characteristic of the modernist avant-garde than of classical realism. Its calculated shifts between prosaic story details and poetic montage passages produce internal, dialectical conflicts rather than narrative coherence. Such characteristics help explain the film's critical reception. They may also explain its lackluster earnings. Audience members may well have been troubled by the film's avant-garde quality. That might explain why *The End of St Petersburg*'s market performance paled in comparison to that of his prior revolutionary work, *The Mother*. The earlier film had the more coherent narrative design and integrated style, and it enjoyed a kinder public reception. *The End of St Petersburg* seemed like an experimental work by comparison, and it paid the price in its commercial release.

Career Consequences

The public response to *The End of St Petersburg* did not appreciably disrupt Pudovkin's career progress. He retained his status as Mezhrabpom's prestige director. In 1928, shortly after the release of *The End of St Petersburg*, he got the opportunity to work on another major production, *Storm Over Asia*. In developing this film on the Mongolian revolution, Pudovkin applied some lessons from the mixed reaction to *The End of St Petersburg*. He adapted the more cohesive narrative design of the sort found in *The Mother* to his film on Mongolia. And rather than shifting back and forth between competing styles, Pudovkin allowed *Storm Over Asia*'s montage passages, including the famous climax with the metaphorical storm, to develop organically out of the drama. The goal was narrative clarity and commensurate popular appeal. *Storm Over Asia* even underwent audience test-surveys with schoolchildren to ensure that they could easily comprehend the film and appreciate its messages; the surveys produced favorable results, with children from various backgrounds indicating that they enjoyed and understood the movie.[9]

Pudovkin was not ready to abandon an experimental inclination in 1928, however. The prospect of sound cinema – already introduced in the West but still on the horizon for Soviet film-makers – suggested new potential for montage innovations. Pudovkin co-authored with Eisenstein and Grigori Alexandrov a 'Statement on Sound', a polemic on behalf the contrapuntal use of sound.[10] Sound counterpoint promised to preserve the dynamism of the montage aesthetic through a sound/image dialectic, offering another possible ingredient of a modernist aesthetic mix. The USSR's slow implementation of sound technology delayed the opportunity to put such ideas to the test, however. Pudovkin was not able to follow through on his ambition of sound montage until 1933 with the production of *Deserter* [Dezertir], in which he undertook some impressive experiments in sound/image counterpoint.

Nevertheless, early 1928 was a heady time for Pudovkin, Eisenstein and the other left film-makers. The 1927 anniversary had occasioned the production of two of the USSR's most sophisticated exercises in film form, *October* and *The End of St Petersburg*, and other experimental films appeared on the Soviet film horizon in early 1928, including Dovzhenko's highly elliptical *Zvenigora*, and Vertov's montage documentary *The Eleventh Year* [Odinnadsatyi]. What is more, the Soviet film industry had developed to the point where it could reduce its dependence on foreign and commercial film revenues.[11] The left Soviet directors might have envisioned a future in which the dilemma of commercial versus political pressures would finally be resolved. With a healthy domestic film industry, the burden on film-makers to produce box-office successes could be reduced, and the left directors might have anticipated that their studios had the financial resources to support ambitious montage films, including more exercises in formal experimentation of the sort represented by *The End of St Petersburg*.

But early 1928 would also see the start of major changes in the Soviet cinema that would alter such ambitions – and much else. This was the beginning of the Soviet Cultural Revolution, during which period the Stalin regime implemented tighter controls on artistic expression. And the nation also moved into the first Five-Year Plan in economic matters, when NEP was phased out in favor of central planning. The transition period would ultimately last four years, until 1932. By the end of that time, state management of cinema affairs would be fully implemented under the regime of central planning, and state-endorsed formulas of artistic practice would take shape under the banner of Soviet Socialist Realism. In the meantime, the conditions under which films like *The End of St Petersburg* were judged changed significantly.

The portent of these changes was a plan announced in early 1928 for the USSR's first-ever Party Conference on Cinema, which was to be held in March. The conference would be overseen by Communist Party officials who would review the state of the Soviet film industry. That review eventually led to the industry's move away from NEP toward central planning and toward more stringent governmental control of film content.[12] Meanwhile the climate of reception for avant-garde films like *October* and *The End of St Petersburg* was changing. The debate about commercial versus ideological films that had endured through the cinema's NEP period was shifting toward another issue, 'intelligible' versus 'unintelligible' films. The troubling track record of montage films in public release raised concerns about whether such movies actually were useful instruments of mass enlightenment. Their disjunctive formal devices seemed to alienate general audiences, and even to leave some spectators genuinely confused. If Soviet cinema was to lead the masses toward greater cultural enlightenment, the films would have to be 'intelligible to the masses', to cite a phrase that started to inform Soviet discourse on cinema.

Such concerns fed into the formal discussions at the March 1928 conference, and *October* came in for particular scrutiny, in part because of the timing of its release on the eve of the conference and in part because of the film's abstract passages. Its critics complained about its allegedly 'bewildering' design and cited claims that worker audiences actually slept through the film even though it was supposed to contribute to their political education. *October* became the immediate lightning rod for complaints about abstraction in montage films, and those complaints continued beyond the conference to circulate in the Soviet press. In this climate, *The End of St Petersburg* escaped the most severe criticism. Pudovkin's film may have seemed reasonably accessible in immediate comparison with Eisenstein's anniversary film, and it was Eisenstein who drew the fire. Pudovkin, to his credit, did not exploit the *October* controversy for invidious professional gain at Eisenstein's expense. Pudovkin publicly praised *October*'s most innovative ingredient, its use of intellectual montage, and acknowledged its influence on his own work. And, as noted above, he even joined with Eisenstein and Alexandrov in August 1928, five months after the conference, in the 'Statement on Sound'. Such gestures might suggest solidarity with Eisenstein as well as a continuing commitment to the kind of modernist sensibility on display in both *October* and *The End of St Petersburg*.[13]

Nevertheless, the troubled initial reception of *The End of St Petersburg* left it open to charges that it was too complex for the Soviet mass audience. And such charges would start to take shape throughout 1928 and 1929. *The End of St Petersburg* would be grouped with *October* and several newer avant-garde works – including Dovzhenko's *Zvenigora* and *The Arsenal*, Grigori Kozintsev and Leonid Trauberg's *The New Babylon* [Novyi Vavilon, 1929], and Vertov's *The Man with the Movie Camera* [Chelovek s kinoapparatom, 1929] – as self-indulgent exercises in aesthetic formalism.[14] Critics of the montage style became more vocal as the Cultural Revolution took shape and the Party leadership encouraged official condemnation of the USSR's entire artistic avant-garde. By early 1930, Dovzhenko's montage film *Earth* [Zemlia] became the object of a Kremlin-sanctioned attack in the pages of *Izvestiia*, and the community of montage film-makers began to sense that they would have to change their practices.[15]

What this was all pointing toward was the eventual formation of the Party-approved aesthetic system of Socialist Realism. As is well known, some montage directors, including Eisenstein, Dovzhenko and Vertov, had difficulty adjusting to the new standards of the 1930s, and their later careers suffered long hiatuses. But another cinema cohort, including such figures as Barnet and Protazanov, made the transition more easily. Those directors who had seemed to be too commercial during the NEP era had something that allowed their work to be received more positively some years later under the terms defined by Socialist Realism. That something may have been a capacity for clear storytelling, precisely the quality that had assured their work commercial success under NEP. Their proven continuity practices certainly did offer ease of narrative comprehension and thus promised to be 'intelligible to the masses'.

Once formalized in the 1930s, the conventions of Socialist Realism in cinema included the ingredients of positive heroes, optimistic plot formulas and linear narratives. But they also included continuity practices. The classical Hollywood system had become a transnational film vernacular by the 1930s. Its protocols of linear plot development, character-based causality and continuity editing seemed to provide narrative clarity in all genres and in any number of international settings. These protocols were duly incorporated into the Soviet cinema system of Socialist Realism.[16] Little wonder that Vertov, a radical critic of linear narrative, would suffer under the regime of Socialist Realism, while Barnet, a Kuleshov Workshop veteran who understood continuity practices, would enjoy a productive later career working within Socialist Realism's stylistic norms.

And how did Pudovkin make the transition? What effect did the legacy of such formalist films as *The End of St Petersburg* have on his subsequent work and on its reception? Pudovkin, I submit, could make the transition reasonably well precisely because of some features already present in his early work and prominent in certain parts of *The End of St Petersburg*, namely a capacity for character-centered narration and the continuity style.

Although Pudovkin was publicly identified as a left, montage director through the late 1920s, his style was never as disjunctive as that of Eisenstein or Vertov, for example. It was easier for Pudovkin to escape the 'formalism' reproach during the heated debates of the Cultural Revolution. In fact, Eisenstein may have done Pudovkin the favor of identifying his colleague as an early believer in continuity. In a famous 1929 anecdote (see Introduction), Eisenstein aligned Pudovkin's editing with concepts of serial linkage and his own with conflict: '"Series"–P[udovkin] and "Collision–E[isenstein]"'.[17] And, as we have seen, Pudovkin's most complicated exercise in film form, *The End of St Petersburg*, escaped the most damning association with the formalism pejorative because of its fortuitous connection to *October*; the latter received the heavy criticism and Pudovkin's equivalent work slipped through the anti-formalism campaign relatively unscathed.

As a result, Pudovkin could reinterpret his own work and revise his thinking about film form during the Cultural Revolution somewhat more easily than could other montage directors. Pudovkin reformulated many of his stated views on cinema so as to identify his work with a realist rather than a modernist sensibility. For example, he wrote of the need for scenarios to be designed so as to promote a greater sense of realism through emotional nuance.[18] He also retreated from his famous 1928 proclamation on sound counterpoint by noting that sound and image could be unified 'through their semantic interaction [rather than] primitive naturalistic unity'.[19] In 1931, he even went through the political education preparatory to becoming a member of the Communist Party. Among other things, the political education would have involved the doctrine that artists should not simply follow personal instincts in creative affairs but should conform to the larger social good as defined by the best wisdom of the Party. That meant making such adjustments in their film technique as would be necessary to meet Party mandates on 'intelligible' film practices.[20]

Such gestures coincided with a genuine effort on Pudovkin's part to develop a precise, legible film style that would contribute to the larger goal of a true mass cinema. In a sense, that had always been his ambition, dating from his first explorations of film technique under Kuleshov's guidance. And Pudovkin's experiences in the later 1920s, including the reception of his silent features, guided him in revising his conception of what actually *would* constitute a film style offering universal legibility. He could measure the public and critical response to his more unified narrative features, *The Mother* and *Storm Over Asia*, against the reception of his most multifaceted film, *The End of St Petersburg*. The latter seemed to offer the least appeal to general audiences. The film's critical reception also suggested that this poor showing may have resulted from that film's apparent fragmentation. Concepts of stylistic unity rather than modernist hybridity would guide Pudovkin's thinking through his later career.

He would never make another film quite like *The End of St Petersburg*; that is, he would never make another film that combined such disparate styles. His later films conformed more to norms of the classical style, and the montage aesthetic was gradually subordinated to requirements of narrative continuity.[21] As the 1930s progressed, he developed theories that stressed clear character development, ultimately embracing Stanislavsky's principles of characterization. Pudovkin's ideas on film form evolved to the point where he called for redundant strategies of film articulation instead of contrapuntal devices; he argued that sound, *mise-en-scène*, editing and acting should reinforce each other to make perfectly clear ideological points for spectators.[22]

A particular combination of circumstance in the mid-1920s encouraged the eclectic film experiment that was *The End of St Petersburg*. A few years earlier or later, and that combination would not have obtained. But in 1926–27, Pudovkin had both the opportunity to measure the audience appeal of the classical style (and he had the opportunity to master it), and the chance to see the potential of the then-novel film technique of intellectual montage. The result was a film that drew from these differing styles and openly exploited the dynamic conflict between them. Intellectual montage would not survive into the Stalin era in its pure form. What would survive would be the classical style, reformulated under the guise of Socialist Realism. And in this there is to be found an important connection between *The End of St Petersburg* and later Pudovkin films. The smooth continuity of the interpersonal scenes in *The End of St Petersburg*, the convincing psychological detail of its principal characters, the narrative that takes account of individual human agency: all these ingredients anticipate conventions of Socialist Realism. Not coincidentally, they also anticipate Pudovkin's later work, and they owe a common debt to his original interest in classical Hollywood.

Long-term Judgments

By the time sustained evaluations of Pudovkin's work began to appear in Soviet and Western publications, they were inflected, in one way or the other, by Pudovkin's association with a realist aesthetic. His emerging identity as a proponent of linear narration, psychologically realistic characters and continuity may even have affected the critical standing of the earlier films such as *The End of St Petersburg*, as though the silent films were judged in light of the later outcomes of Pudovkin's career. *The End of St Petersburg* proved particularly difficult to appreciate because it did not fit comfortably into the realist model.

By the mid-1930s, Pudovkin's early work was being re-evaluated by Soviet critics according to the norms of Socialist Realism. Such critics imposed the evaluative standards of the 1930s retroactively on the cinema of the 1920s. A characteristic example appears in a 1935 book on Soviet cinema that was prepared for foreign publication and was thus intended officially to proclaim to the world the wisdom of the USSR's commitment to Socialist Realism. In this vein, Pudovkin's early films warranted retroactive praise for their early signs of realism, especially in the realm of characterization. Pudovkin's work represents 'a consistently realistic school interested in the heroes of the film[s] and in their psychology'. His montage practices do not overwhelm the character-centered narratives, according to this view, but are subordinated to his 'dramaturgical principle' of realistic character development.[23] In this spirit, even *The End of St Petersburg* earns praise, not because of its formal properties, but because of its convincing portraits of the film's central characters: 'Pudovkin possesses a remarkable gift for selecting his actors' ensemble and for working with them.'[24]

The first major Russian studies of Pudovkin's work were written in this Stalinist intellectual climate of retroactive appraisal. Such studies impose a teleology on Pudovkin's career: his early work is represented as a search eventually to find a realist aesthetic, which would finally be realized in the 1930s through his commitment to Socialist Realism. The silent films warrant praise to the extent that they anticipate the later realist norms and condemnation to the extent that they betrayed signs of self-indulgent formalism. *The Mother* holds up best under such *ex post facto* standards; it had the benefit of manifest psychological realism and a positive central character (and a source novel that was in the literary canon of Socialist Realism). *The End of St Petersburg* was to prove more troubling, according to such Stalinism norms. Its episodic form and frequent exercises in intellectual montage diminish its value as a representation of the Bolshevik Revolution. The capstone of this line of argument is Alexander Mariamov's 1951 book on Pudovkin. He finds that *The End of St Petersburg* contains numerous aesthetic 'mistakes' which impede Pudovkin's progress toward Socialist Realism, namely its abstract montage passages. Other ingredients, including its character-centered subplots, more closely approximate later aesthetic standards. Despite the tepid evaluation, Mariamov opines that the film's contributions outweigh its liabilities by virtue of the fact that in its best ingredients 'we are able to recognize the [eventual] triumph of the methods of Socialist Realism'.[25]

The post-Stalin intellectual environment in the USSR permitted more nuanced accounts of Pudovkin's work, though his association with continuity film-making would still inform discussions of his early work. Histories of Soviet cinema continued to treat Pudovkin as the resident realist among the 1920s montage directors. For example, Yuri Vorontsov and Igor Rachuk in *The Phenomenon of Soviet Cinema* – another official account of Soviet cinema prepared for international consumption – claim that Pudovkin's 1920s montage work manifests a regard for linearity that would carry over to his later work. That in turn provides a connection to the USSR's subsequent norm of cinema realism. This quality distinguishes Pudovkin from some other left directors, including Eisenstein, whose 1920s formal experimentalism often led to aesthetic dead-ends. To Pudovkin's credit, his realist inclinations would endure after the excesses of the left avant-garde were forgotten: 'He [Pudovkin] began to wonder [during the 1920s] if he had given way to traditional tastes instead of renewing cinema and helping it to advance. Today we can see that his doubts were groundless.'[26] In line with this view, *The Mother* and *Storm Over Asia* represent the great achievements of Pudovkin's silent film career. In the more complex *The End of St Petersburg*, Pudovkin simply 'paid his due to "left" poetics'.[27]

As Western critics fashioned their image of Pudovkin's work, they had available his dual incarnations as both a montage innovator and as a proponent of classical realism. The fact that his silent films involved character-based stories and that he eventually embraced the classical system shaped Western views of Pudovkin, no less than those propagated by the Soviets. The most common way to characterize Pudovkin has been to compare him with Eisenstein and then to distinguish between these two most celebrated practitioners of the montage style. Eisenstein inevitably is adjudged to have advanced the more radical style, especially in the dialectical montage on display in *The Battleship Potemkin*; Pudovkin's inclinations toward continuity makes him the more formally conservative figure, according to this standard.

Pudovkin's earliest Western admirers were linked to the 'left modernist' school of the late 1920s and 1930s. Critics in such leftist film journals as *Close Up* and *Experimental Cinema* looked to the Soviet montage cinema to provide positive models of film practice on both political and formal grounds. While condemning Hollywood for commercialism and formulaic storytelling, these writers praised the progressive messages and experimental style of Soviet montage films. Eisenstein was easy to embrace for these true believers. Pudovkin presented a more complicated matter. He was clearly a left, montage director, but his thinking about cinema betrayed debts to Hollywood classicism, especially in his representation of film characters. Pudovkin's most ardent supporters found ways to recast this aspect of his work as a sign of an experimental modernism. The American Marxist Harry Potamkin wrote in *Experimental Cinema* that Pudovkin's film characters represented a distillation of larger social conditions. They embodied the historical situation of revolutionary Russia. Unlike the more helpless victims of social injustice to be found in such films as F. W. Murnau's *The Last Laugh* [Der Letzte Mann, 1924], Pudovkin's characters represented the 'concentration of the social force'. And the alternating narrative scales of *The End of St Petersburg* constituted an innovative example of dialectical art; the film portrayed the dynamic interaction of society and the individual.[28]

Some of Pudovkin's European admirers found another way to celebrate his work and to distinguish it from that of his fellow Russian montage directors. They identified a 'lyrical', 'poetic' or sometimes 'musical' strain in Pudovkin's work. Pudovkin's silent films manifested a flow and a grace in their designs that differentiated them from the more elliptical techniques of Eisenstein or Vertov. The greater sense of linearity in Pudovkin's editing encouraged the claim that his style manifested a quality of lyricism; Eisenstein's disjunctive editing, by contrast, worked through jarring effects. French critic Léon Moussinac distinguished between Eisenstein and Pudovkin by use of a single trope. 'A film by Eisenstein resembles a scream, and a film by Pudovkin evokes a song,' he wrote in a 1928 monograph on Soviet cinema.[29]

The musical analogy seemed to apply most readily to *The Mother*. Its narrative design – starting small and opening up in evenly-paced stages – evinced elegance and harmony. Its graceful unfolding warranted comparison with a Beethoven-like sense of musical rhythm and balance.[30] But what about *The End of St Petersburg*, with its multiple sub-plots and many stylistic shifts? In line with this lyricism argument, *The End of St Petersburg* is not so much a modernist mix, as it is a poeticized rendering of history. The poeticism resides in certain of the movie's stylistic flourishes rather than in its overall design. Pudovkin's montage takes historical reality and then renders it in an abstract manner. And mundane objects of physical reality take on new, poeticized qualities when depicted through the oblique angles and rapid cuts of a Pudovkin montage passage. Still, the lyricism paradigm forced such critics to conclude that *The End of St Petersburg* was simply less successful than *The Mother*, as though Pudovkin was striving for a harmonious design in *The End of St Petersburg* but failed to achieve it, realizing true lyricism only in particular passages.[31]

The Eisenstein–Pudovkin comparison was most explicitly put forth in Dwight Macdonald's influential writings on early Soviet film. In fact, his often-anthologized 1931 essay 'Eisenstein, Pudovkin and Others' may have provided the model for how Soviet silent cinema would be described in later English-language film history textbooks.[32] Macdonald identifies Eisenstein and Pudovkin as the two leading lights of Russian cinema and suggests that a comparison of their methods provides a useful summary of the montage style's overall potential. He then notes Eisenstein's capacity for mass dramas and Pudovkin's predilection for personalized stories. Eisenstein earns higher praise because his more intense, densely-packed montage is somehow truer to cinema's essence as a visual medium, according to Macdonald. By contrast, Pudovkin's more linear editing and storytelling evoke a novelistic tradition: 'Where Eisenstein cinematizes, Pudovkin narrates. The "shock-linkage" contrast sketched out by Eisenstein between his point of view and that of Pudovkin is remarkably accurate. Though Pudovkin builds his pictures around certain key scenes, he links them together in a time relationship instead of letting them conflict in space. His pictures are more literary, less cinematic in form.'[33] Macdonald's emphasis on linearity makes it difficult for him to account for the digressive narration employed in *The End of St Petersburg*. He is left to conclude that the film's 'action ... is complicated by the inevitable scope and detail of historical events in an advanced civilization, and is therefore broken up into shorter and more numerous episodes'.[34]

Variants of this evaluation of Pudovkin survived through the decades in film history texts. Such widely read volumes would have popularized the terms under which Pudovkin was understood in the West.[35] They did so by drawing together and consolidating the various motifs that were already available in the Western literature. The chapters on Soviet silent cinema in such synoptic histories commonly feature Eisenstein–Pudovkin comparisons; and the familiar conflict versus linkage, mass hero versus individual, and even 'scream' versus 'song' differentiations figure in those accounts. The image of Pudovkin as the advocate of linear narrative is better sustained by the example of *The Mother* than by *The End of St Petersburg* in such summary chapters. As a consequence, the former film receives more attention in these overviews of Pudovkin's silent career. *The End of St Petersburg* proves harder to reconcile with Pudovkin's image as the advocate of sequential narration, and the film's relative eclecticism must be explained away. In one of the most perceptive such accounts, for example, David Cook praises *The Mother* as a 'beautifully proportioned film' and explains the elements of abstraction in *The End of St Petersburg* by suggesting (correctly) that it most resembles Eisenstein's work.[36]

Many of the more specialized studies emerging from modern academic film studies have refined this view of Pudovkin as the teller of linear tales without necessarily challenging its premises. For example, Paul

Burns, in an essay on Pudovkin's silent films, uses Eisenstein's 'linkage' dictum as his starting point, asserting that the concept of 'linkage seems [to be] an apt description of Pudovkin's personal vision'.[37] In line with this premise, Burns treats the silent features, including *The End of St Petersburg*, as models of narrative and thematic unity. Murray Smith in a study of characterization in Soviet silent films finds cause to connect *The End of St Petersburg* with later practices of Socialist Realism. He notes that the film's three central characters anticipate Socialist Realism's standard ensemble of character types.[38]

The analytical conventions for discussing Pudovkin thus seem to have held strong from at least the 1930s until recent times. But two new and sophisticated studies of Pudovkin's silent cinema take a different tack. Both Amy Sargeant in the first book-length study of Pudovkin's silent films in English and Panayiota Mini, in a dissertation covering similar terrain, reinsert Pudovkin into the context of 1920s modernism. That framework allows them to understand *The End of St Petersburg* as something other than an eclectic curiosity.[39] For Sargeant, Pudovkin's silent movies represent an avant-garde sensibility rather than being the precursors of a realist style. She identifies various of Pudovkin's sources in the modernist intellectual climate of the early twentieth century, including scientific discourses. This research allows her to appraise *The End of St Petersburg* in the light of psychological theories that dealt with the dynamic of the individual and society. Mini performs a similar inquiry into Pudovkin's intellectual sources, and explores the extent to which Pudovkin incorporates Soviet tenets of political economy into his films. This inquiry allows her to analyze *The End of St Petersburg* as an artistic text that gives sophisticated dramatic form to Soviet theories of socio-economic development. Both studies are able to recover the historical pre-conditions of *The End of St Petersburg*, especially in the intellectual history of early twentieth-century Russia, and they appraise the film in that context, rather than imposing a retroactive standard of realism.

These two studies set the current standard for further inquiry into Pudovkin's work in general and *The End of St Petersburg* in particular. However, the fact that they are not constrained by the conventional view that Pudovkin was a realist-in-the-making does not necessarily undermine the traditional emphasis on linearity in Pudovkin's work. That enduring paradigm did and does provide considerable explanatory power for both Pudovkin's silent and sound films – with one important exception, *The End of St Petersburg*. That film never did quite fit the model of tidy linearity that was supposed to be the defining ingredient of Pudovkin's films. The truly dialectical design of *The End of St Petersburg* was rarely recognized or properly praised by film critics because that concept was apparently reserved for Eisenstein.

The film's aesthetic complexity is the mark of Pudovkin's achievement, and that results from his effort to combine ingredients. *The End of St Petersburg* is a messy masterpiece. Its brilliance results from Pudovkin's disparate stylistic borrowings and from his refusal to try somehow to fuse those styles into a seamless whole. In the best spirit of the avant-garde, Pudovkin allows the seams to show through. As a result, *The End of St Petersburg* amply rewards subsequent viewings, seams and all.

Notes

1. Jay Leyda, *Kino: A History of the Russian and Soviet Film* (3rd edn), Princeton, NJ, 1983, pp. 235–6.

2. This information comes from movie advertisement pages in *Izvestiia*, 7 November–14 December 1927.

3. Iu. A. L'vunin, 'Organizatsiia Mezhdunarodnaia Rabochaia Pomoshch' i sovetskoe kino (1921–1936 gg.)', *Vestnik Moskovskogo Universiteta*, 9, no. 4 (1971), p. 33, n. 90.

4. Ibid., pp. 33–4.

5. *Izvestiia*, 30 December 1927, p. 5; *Pravda*, 9 November 1927, p. 5.

6. *Kino-front*, 1928, no. 1, pp. 16–18; *Trud*, 3 November 1927, p. 6.

7. *Novyi Lef*, 1927, nos 11/12, pp. 29–33; available in translation in Richard Taylor and Ian Christie (eds), *The Film Factory: Russian and Soviet Cinema in Documents, 1896–1939*, Cambridge, MA, 1988, pp. 180–3 (subsequent quotations from this text).

8. Ibid., p. 180.

9. Panayiota Mini, 'Pudovkin's Cinema of the 1920s', PhD dissertation, University of Wisconsin-Madison, 2002, p. 351.

10. Available in translation in S. M. Eisenstein, *Selected Works, Volume I: Writings, 1922–34*, ed. and trans. Richard Taylor, London and Bloomington, IN, 1988, pp. 113–14.

11. Vance Kepley, Jr, 'The Origins of Soviet Cinema: A Study in Industry Development', *Quarterly Review of Film Studies*, 10, no. 1 (1985), pp. 34–5.

12. See Richard Taylor, *The Politics of Soviet Cinema, 1917–1929*, Cambridge, 1979, ch. 6 on Party intervention and the 1928 conference.

13. On the *October* debates, see documents in Taylor and Christie (eds), *Film Factory*, pp. 198–200, 216–35.

14. For an example of such public attacks on the montage style, see ibid., pp. 259–62.

15. *Izvestiia*, 4 April 1930, p. 2.

16. I have tried to make this argument about Socialist Realism and the classical Hollywood style in Kepley, 'Pudovkin, Socialist Realism, and the Classical

Hollywood Style', *Journal of Film and Video*, 47, no. 4 (1995–96), pp. 3–16. Among other scholars who find connections between popular cinema formulas and the cinema of Socialist Realism are: Ian Christie, 'Introduction', in Taylor and Christie (eds), *Film Factory*, pp. 1–17; and Richard Taylor, 'A "Cinema of the Millions": Soviet Socialist Realism and the Problem of Film Comedy', *Journal of Contemporary History*, 18 (1983), pp. 439–61; Taylor, 'Boris Shumyatsky and the Soviet Cinema in the 1930s: Ideology as Mass Entertainment', *Historical Journal of Film, Radio, and Television*, 6 (1986), pp. 43–64.

17. Eisenstein, *Selected Works*, p. 144.

18. Vsevolod Pudovkin, 'Scenario and Direction', *Experimental Cinema*, no. 3 (1931), pp. 16–18.

19. Vsevolod Pudovkin, 'The Role of Sound', in Taylor and Christie (eds), *Film Factory*, p. 329.

20. A. I. Rubailo, *Partiinoe rukovodstvo razvitiem kinoiskusstva (1928–1937 gg.)*, Moscow, 1976, p. 77.

21. *Deserter* provides the exception to this general claim. Its innovative use of sound does represent a reformulation of Pudovkin's avant-garde ambitions. His subsequent sound films would conform more and more to norms of continuity.

22. See Kepley, 'Pudovkin, Socialist Realism', p. 306.

23. N. Yesuitov, 'Basic Trends in Soviet Film Art', in A. Arossev (ed.), *Soviet Cinema*, Moscow, 1935, p. 63.

24. Ibid., p. 64.

25. Alexander Mar'iamov, *Narodnyi artist SSSR Vsevolod Pudovkin*, Moscow, 1951, p. 89 (German-language edition, *Pudowkin: Kampf und Vollendung*, trans. Ruth Brückner, Berlin, 1954, p. 179). Earlier Stalinist studies include Nikolai Iezuitov, *Vsevolod Pudovkin*, Moscow, 1937 and L. Rusanova, *Vsevolod Pudovkin*, Moscow, 1939.

26. Yuri Vorontsev and Igor Rachuk, *The Phenomenon of Soviet Cinema*, trans. Doris Bradbury, Moscow, 1980, p. 49.

27. Ibid., p. 52.

28. Harry Potamkin, 'Film Problems of Soviet Russia', *Experimental Cinema*, 1, no. 1 (1930), p. 4; and Potamkin, 'Populism and Dialectics', *Experimental Cinema*, 1, no. 2 (1930), p. 17.

29. Léon Moussinac, *Le Cinéma soviétique*, Paris, 1928, p. 161.

30. Luda and Jean Schnitzer, *Vsevolod Pudovkine*, Paris, 1966, pp. 30–1.

31. Ibid., p. 35.

32. The essay first appeared in the March 1931 issue of *Miscellany*. It is reprinted in Lewis Jacobs (ed.), *The Emergence of Film Art*, New York, 1969, pp. 122–46 (subsequent quotations from this edition).

33. Ibid., pp. 136–7.

34. Ibid., p. 144.

35. For a representative sample of these synoptic accounts see: Arthur Knight, *The Liveliest Art* (rev. edn), New York, 1979, pp. 65–85; Gerald Mast, *A Short*

History of the Movies (2nd edn), Indianapolis, IN, 1976, ch. 8; David Cook, *A History of Narrative Film* (2nd edn), New York, 1990, ch. 5.

36. Cook, *History*, pp. 195–6.

37. Paul Burns, 'Linkage: Pudovkin's Classics Revisited', *Journal of Popular Film and Television*, 9, no. 2 (1981), p. 70.

38. Murray Smith, 'The Influence of Socialist Realism on Soviet Montage: *The End of St Petersburg*, *Fragment of an Empire*, and *Arsenal*', *Journal of Ukrainian Studies*, 19, no. 1 (1994), pp. 45–66.

39. Amy Sargeant, *Vsevolod Pudovkin: Classic Films of the Soviet Avant-Garde*, London and New York, 2000, ch. 4; Mini, 'Pudovkin's Cinema', ch. 5.

Further Reading

Soviet Silent Cinema

Bryher, Winifred, *Film Problems of Soviet Russia*, London, 1929.

Gillespie, David, *Early Soviet Cinema: Innovation, Ideology and Propaganda*, London, 2000.

Kenez, Peter, *Cinema and Soviet Society – From the Revolution to the Death of Stalin*, London and New York, 2000.

Leyda, Jay, *Kino: A History of the Russian and Soviet Film* (3rd edn), Princeton, NJ, 1983.

Taylor, Richard, *The Politics of the Soviet Cinema, 1917–1929*, Cambridge, 1979.

Taylor, Richard and Ian Christie (eds), *The Film Factory: Russian and Soviet Cinema in Documents, 1896–1939*, Cambridge, MA, 1988.

Youngblood, Denise, *Soviet Cinema of the Silent Era, 1918–1935*, Ann Arbor, MI, 1985.

— *Movies for the Masses: Popular Cinema and Soviet Society in the 1920s*, Cambridge, 1992.

Pudovkin and *The End of St Petersburg*

Burns, Paul, 'Linkage: Pudovkin's Classics Revisited', *Journal of Popular Film and Television*, 9, no. 2 (1981), pp. 70–7.

Dart, Peter, *Pudovkin's Films and Film Theory*, Ann Arbor, MI, 1974.

Kepley, Vance, Jr, 'Pudovkin and the Classical Hollywood Tradition', *Wide Angle*, 7, no. 3 (1985), pp. 54–61.

— 'Pudovkin and the Continuity Style: Problems of Space and Narration', *Discourse*, 17, no. 3 (1995), pp. 85–100.

Mini, Panayiota, 'Pudovkin's Cinema of the 1920s', PhD disseration, University of Wisconsin-Madison, 2002.

Petrić, Vlada, 'Vsevolod Pudovkin', in Richard Roud (ed.), *Cinema: A Critical Dictionary*, New York, 1980, Vol. 2, pp. 800–7.

Pudovkin, V. I., *Film Technique and Film Acting*, trans. and ed. Ivor Montagu, New York, 1970.

Sargeant, Amy, *Vsevolod Pudovkin: Classic Films of the Soviet Avant-Garde*, London and New York, 2000.

Smith, Murray, 'The Influence of Socialist Realism on Soviet Montage: *The End of St. Petersburg, Fragment of an Empire*, and *Arsenal*', *Journal of Ukrainian Studies*, 19, no. 1 (1994), pp. 45–65.

Sorlin, Pierre, *The Film in History: Restaging the Past*, Oxford, 1980, ch. 7.